JENE :

Rail Dogs

Wesley Zolecki

See you on the road!

This book is dedicated to my late grandmother, Marie Sauerberg, for teaching me unconditional love, patience, and compassion; and my best friend Evan Quackenbush. I would like to thank every person who was a part of this story for the impact they had on my heart and soul.

CONTENTS

PART 1-
THE PLAN

It was a decision reached unanimously and instantaneously on an early summer road trip from Nashville, Tennessee towards Allentown, Pennsylvania where we would be working for the summer. My best friend Evan Quackenbush and I were driving together. And yes, that's really his last name. I have known the Norwegian since the fourth grade. We met when I moved to a new elementary school in Prairie Grove, Illinois, a small village about thirty miles northwest of Chicago. For my tenth birthday present that year Evan gave me a button that said, "Is that your face or did your neck throw up?" The maturity level of our humor has only slightly evolved since that birthday.

We made our pact while driving through Eastern Tennessee and the Great Smokey Mountains. I sat behind the wheel of my family's fourteen-year-old, slightly rusty, maroon Buick Century. Evan was in the passenger seat keeping me entertained as the car weaved swiftly and gracefully through the forested peaks. It was a warm, bright Friday afternoon and a mystical feeling overcame me as sunshine painted the fluid waves of rolling foliage and rock formations. Never having driven through the mountains before, the popping of my eardrums as we climbed and descended left me light-headed and slightly high. The six-cylinder fuel injection engine of the Buick revved and groaned like a fatigued lawnmower as it fought valiantly against the hills of Interstate 40. The excitement in the air was palpable.

We had just finished our sophomore year of college, Evan at the University of Illinois in Champaign-Urbana, and I at Marquette University in Milwaukee, Wisconsin. This road trip was part of the process of participating in a summer internship with The Southwestern Company, selling educational books and software door-to-door. It was to be my second venture into the societal abyss that is door-to-door sales. Evan was my lone recruit, whom I would manage, train, and whose general well-being I would more or less be responsible for throughout the summer. The first week was spent in Nashville at sales school, an emotionally draining yet powerful training seminar in success and sales principles. Here we learned everything we would need to run our own business for the summer.

Sales school takes place in the heart of downtown at the War Memorial, an old theater with about a thousand seats filled with highly motivated, enthusiastic college students. Sales managers, motivational speakers, and the president of the company spoke to us about integrity, hard work, goal setting, and commitment. All the principles that would help us not only to be successful in running a small direct sales business for the summer, but for the rest of our lives. Every day we left the auditorium feeling invigorated about the opportunity that lay before us; the chance to become entrepreneurs, accomplished salespeople, and better, more rounded human beings.

The greatest challenge of the weeklong training was learning an extensive sales talk to be delivered word for word in front of prospective customers. The next greatest challenge was coping with the fact that you would be working and living half way across the country in a foreign environment knocking on doors 80 hours a week on straight commission. Lastly, when you left Nashville you had no idea where you would be living for the summer. Upon arrival in our "territory" we would begin searching for host families through churches, community organizations, and mostly by knocking on doors asking families if they might have leads for housing. It was our job as experienced managers to instill confidence in our recruits by staying positive and pretending we were not scared shitless ourselves. Our personal organization was composed of a total of forty student managers and first-year students from Wisconsin, Illinois and Iowa. On Friday morning, with our brains packed full of information and nervous excitement peaked, we ventured eastward in a car caravan toward Pennsylvania.

The monumental decision was that upon graduation from college in a year (and a summer) from this date, we would backpack together through Europe. I do not remember how the idea came to us, or if it was beamed down supernaturally through our collective spiritual consciousness, but the seemingly casual commitment immediately became chiseled in stone as our most certain future. Prior to this trip, Evan and I had not been strangers to adventure, getting into our share of mischief together throughout our formative years. One such example was the time I stole an Andes candy mint from our permanent substitute teacher's lunchbox in the fifth grade while Evan distracted her with a bogus question about our math homework. I was such a brat I even went through the trouble of putting the empty wrapper back inside. Another time was when we ditched a shared cab in Milwaukee one drunken college night, running away excitedly after launching our beer bottles into the air for no apparent reason. Evan and I always seemed to be more daring and boisterous when we were together. I guess we bring out the best and the worst in one other, just as best friends should do.

A journey across the pond to wreak havoc and to plunder as adults seemed like a perfectly natural progression. Evan had been abroad once during a junior high student program in which he spent a week and a half in England and France. His impression of the continent was as an endless litany of history, culture, and possibility. It would be my second time. I had studied for a semester in Oxford, England my junior year of college. I had truly cherished the experience of traveling by myself on the mid-semester break to Florence and Rome in Italy, and San Sebastian and Madrid in Spain. I stayed with two friends who were studying abroad in Florence and San Sebastian and found cheap hotels to stay in the two capital cities. I remember brimming over with nervous energy when waiting in the middle of the night for a train from Bologna to Florence, watching backpackers sleeping on their bags, looking so free and untamed. Most of them were unshaven and had not showered in a few days. They seemed to know what they were doing, but I was freaked out. The station wasn't very clean and I was unsure of its safety at that hour of the night. Surely I was an easy target for a mugging, walking around like a lost puppy. All the instructions at the ticket machine were written in Italian and it was rejecting my credit card. I had no one to turn to for help but myself. Eventually I found someone to help me use the machine and ended up having an amazing trip. Overcoming my fear of the dark, lonely train station left me confident that I could handle the uncertainty of foreign travel. With a solid companion like Evan by my side I would be unstoppable.

So it was written, after senior year and one more summer of raising capital through selling books, we would embark on the trip of our lives throughout Western Europe. Riding the rails, seeing the sights, drinking the local drinks, and sampling the regional deli-cacies. This journey would be our ultimate introduction to the world of our history. A vision quest. A chance for us to sow our oats; to indulge intellectual and cultural curiosi-ties on a grand stage. To experiment with alternative states of mind and consciousness. My imagination ran wild as I tried to picture how freeing it would be to roam the continent with just a backpack.

That summer Evan and I grew from being just good buddies to being more like brothers. We lived together with a host family we had met through a church in the town of Bethlehem, PA. It's an old steel mecca outside of Philadelphia that was booming at the turn of the twentieth century but has now faded into obscurity. This family was kind and caring, but the discomfort of housing four students in their previously quiet old barn house was too much. After a month they kindly asked us to leave. Specifically, they asked us to move out because they said they had found a porn site had been visited on their computer. This was actually my fault. I had not been surfing porn but had clicked on an unknown email link that led to one of these sites. I closed the window immediately but it was too late. Evan told our other roommates we had to leave because I am a pervert. I still insist that this is not the truth.

It turned out for the better though, because I found us a new headquarters in a bigger home where we would have a whole basement to ourselves. The Gough family had two friendly high school kids and a beautiful home in the country. They were one of my first customers that summer. I had called the mom, Laurie, for advice when we were left homeless. She talked it over with her husband Kevin and said they would give it a shot. He was a salesman himself and thought our business was great. He also thought having a keg of beer on tap in his garage was pretty cool too. Many nights after work I would come home and share a couple of drinks and laughs at the kitchen table. This was not advisable behavior for a student leader but Evan did not seem to mind. We had some great nights sitting there telling stories about all the crazy things that would happen to us during the day.

By far the most bizarre experience I had in eight years of selling books occurred just after moving in with the Goughs. It was the day that David, one of the first years in our organization, came to work with me. David was a timid nineteen-year-old fella from the University of Mississippi. He was struggling to make any sales and wanted to see how someone experienced did the job. Everything was going smoothly until we ran across the street from one prospect's house to speak to another who was in his front yard. My car was still sitting in the driveway of the previous family. During the demonstration in I noticed the dad of the last house was trying to leave and I was blocking him. I asked David to run across to move my car for me, which he did, parking it on the street at the top of a big hill. Minutes later I wrapped up my sample case after not making a sale and began to walk back to the car.

"Funny," I thought. The Buick seemed to have been further down the road than I had remembered. In less than a second I deduced that, yes, the car had moved, and yes, it was still moving with no one inside. As it built momentum down the steep hill and out of my sight, I simply continued my casual pace forward, waiting for the impending tragedy to unfold. David dropped his notepad and began sprinting after the car in vein. I knew it was already too late though. I heard a bump, followed by a few seconds later by a hard crash. It was not until I walked over the hill that I realized exactly what had happened.

Apparently ole David had brilliantly parked the car in neutral. As it had gained steam it had somehow swerved off the street and into someone's front yard, where, judging by the tire tracks, it hopped onto two wheels on the right side of the car. After crashing back to all fours, it redirected itself on a large boulder and headed back into the street. When it crossed back onto the pavement it turned itself again, straightened out and rolled directly into a three-way intersection, smashing into an embankment on the other side of the road. Thanks to divine intervention there were no cars crossing the road at the posted 45 mph. Also, neither of the two men mowing their lawns on tractors were in the way of the Buick's self-destructive final curtsy. Although I was sad about having lost my car, which held so many sentimental memories from childhood, I was more preoccupied with comforting David, who was having a nervous breakdown.

"It's alright," I pleaded. "No one was hurt, that's the most important thing. Just calm down."

I ended up selling the Buick to the scrap yard for $200 after it was considered fully totaled. Obviously David was unable to help pay for my new used car as he had not made any money yet. Despite the challenge, I had my best week of the summer up to that point and finished with the best story in our entire organization.

The next car I bought, a 1988 Pontiac 6000, was running perfectly well until Evan borrowed it to go to the store and ran it into the culvert at the end of the Gough's driveway. I had the front right wheel repaired and then we road tripped back to Nashville. To get back home as quickly as possible we decided to take turns at the wheel and drive through the night taking three-hour shifts. I woke up at one point in the middle of a hot, humid Tennessee afternoon, with Evan behind the wheel, the Pontiac 6000 tearing across the countryside. It took me a moment to come to after my deep, heavy sleep. Shortly after catching my bearings the engine died and the car rolled to a stop, completely empty on gas.

"Well," I said, "looks like you've got to figure this one out."

He accepted responsibility for his mistake and began hitching for a ride to the next gas station. The man that pulled over to pick him up was a jovial middle-aged Native America with a long braided ponytail. He was burning incense as he drove down the highway, perhaps in the midst of a sacred ceremony. The car was an old blue hatchback from the 70s, possibly a Gremlin. I prayed for Evan's safe return, also preparing myself for the possibility that I may never see him again. An hour later, with a nervous sweat on my brow, the smiling Indian man dropped him off and we were back on the highway. If our Europe adventure was to be half as interesting as that summer we would be just fine with that.

Down in Champaign-Urbana in the spring of 2003 we sat at the desk of the local travel agent, committing whole heartedly to our excursion by purchasing airplane and rail tickets. Money may not be able to buy personal freedom, but it came pretty damn close that day. The passes for the train would allow for fifteen days of railway transport, to be determined at our own leisure, valid for nearly every major city in Europe. Our departure date was to be a mere three days after returning to Chicago at the end of the summer. There would be no looking back or room for doubts from this moment for-ward. I wonder if the sales consultant could possibly appreciate the excitement beaming in our eyes, or could hardly imagine the absolute degree of monkey business in which we would be engaging.

Fast forward to the last week of August 2003, which found me in Orange County, California in a mad rush to finish my summer gig and get books delivered and personally demonstrated to all three hundred of my customers from the last three months of selling. More consequently, it found me in an effort to help a first year dealer in our organization, named Heidi, deliver her books in time to return with me back to Nashville. Heidi had a phenomenal first summer in the program and was in a position to finish as the top first year dealer out of about two thousand students across the entire U.S., Canada, and Europe. I was enthused about being able to help her achieve this goal, as I had been coaching and mentoring her all summer to reach her personal best, overcoming the myriad emotional hardships of selling books door-to-door on straight commission. Secondly, I was, as they say in Cali, "hella stoked" to spend time with her outside the confinements of the work environment. She happened to be an extremely attractive firecracker of a blond with a sharp wit and curvaceous, athletic body. I was a smitten kitten.

I remember checking her out at one of our pre-summer meetings back in Milwaukee and being intrigued. We had begun flirting in sales

school. As a student manager I was not supposed to get involved with first year students
romantically. The distraction of romance during the summer can only impede one from their
goals. But I could not help being impressed
by her dogged determination to learn and the
intense focus in her eyes. I knew she was
going to do well in the program and wanted to
help her as much as possible. We talked nearly
every day on the phone that summer, giving
each other pump up calls in the morning before
work. At our weekly Sunday meetings we would
have personal conferences together. I would
listen to her struggles from each week, trying
to help her remain positive and see the big
picture. After three months of total celibacy
and the slow buildup of sexual tension, I
was ready to explode. To say I had developed
a crush would be an understatement; I had
already fallen hard. The fact that I would be
leaving for a two-month trip the next week
did nothing to phase me. Practicality must not
interfere in the pursuit of love.

Selling books with the Southwestern company
was by far the most rewarding experience I
have ever had. It was also the most chal-
lenging. Although educational products are
more appealing to consumers than magazines or
security systems, we still had to overcome the
fact that people just do not like door-to-door

salesmen. Being college students did help open people's minds, as well as the fact that we sold great products. Our flagship product was a three-book set of study guides called the Volume Library, which helps parents refresh their memory on information they have forgotten since they were in school. People got excited about a product that made it easier for them to take interest in their children's studies and feel like they were being good parents. Children benefited from having an extra resource in the home that they could use to be more independent students.

Every day I sat down with fifteen to twenty families, stressing the importance of education, the benefits of college, and the advantages of having the Volume Library. Entering a person's home is a very intimate experience. I learned how to connect with people quickly, remain positive and dynamic, and convince perfect strangers to trust me enough to write a personal check in my name without even receiving the product. I explained to them that upon my return in the fall they would get their products hand delivered and that I would sit down with the kids and show them how to use them. I saw myself as more of an educational consultant than just a door-to-door salesperson.

Delivery week was by far the most intense, stressful portion of the summer. Throughout its course we collected as much money as possible from customers to solidify their orders as well as provide the company with enough money to ship us our books. As independent contractors we were responsible for buying the books on credit. Therefore the company would ship an amount of product based on how many orders we had taken up to that point. The last week of the summer was the time to return with the products in hand hoping customers would have the remaining balance available for us in cash. Because some individuals put down little or no payment in the beginning, it made for an interesting challenge to coax the rest of the money out of them. Especially those who had had three months time to change their minds.

The entire gamut of human behavior was on display during delivery week. People would not answer the door when you knew they were inside, others would say flat out that they did not want the products even though I had already paid for them. Some people were on vacation that week; others had lost their jobs and legitimately did not have the money. Many would ask for extensions on the payment despite my having explained previously that I had to return to school the next week and would not be available to collect money later. Sometimes people had moved. Many others reassured us they would have the money if we came back later in the week. Some did, others proceeded to not answer the door when we returned, even though I knew they were inside. Often times the customers would be mad at me and take out their anger from not being able to afford the books. Being yelled at and criticized by delinquent customers was always a pleasure.

This final week was emotionally taxing to say the least. Having a bad delivery period could affect the overall outcome of your summer by up to 50% of your expected profits. This is when we worked the longest hours, sometimes sixteen hours/day, lugging a heavy box full of books to each door. It took every ounce of energy and patience possible to come out ahead. There were customers whose houses I would drive by over ten times just to try and catch them at home. That being said, the majority of customers were lovely people, happy to see us, waiting excitedly with the money in hand. I would hand out suckers to all the kids and get them enthusiastic about the books and the upcoming school year. I always got a warm feeling and a sense of accomplishment during deliveries. It made the whole summer worthwhile.

It was a perfect coincidence that Evan was wrapping up his summer in Corona, CA just east of Heidi and me, and was ready to leave on the very same day. The universe was conspiring to make this the most memorable summer of my life. The three of us car caravanned the two and a half day drive back to Nashville in separate cars, holding up signs with pictures of giant dicks on them, making humorous gestures back and forth, giving air blow jobs and flicking each other off; anything to try and stay awake and decrease the monotony of spending fourteen hours in a car by ourselves.

At nighttime we would stop at the seediest and accordingly cheapest motels we could possibly find along the Interstate to save our hard earned pesos and give our weary eyes a break from the road. We chose no name towns and motels with neon vacancy signs swinging out front. We checked in with receptionists with names along the lines of Verne and Wilma in Arizona and Oklahoma. These outdated, low rent establishments lent a sense of danger to our road trip. We felt like bandits running on horseback with our loot, racing the sun and the clock. Between the three of us we were carrying in upwards of $50,000 US dollars in cash, check and credit card remittances.

To have your best friend in the car ahead of you and the object of your affection in the car behind, cruising lazily across the great wild west of the United States, with the warm autumn wind whipping across your face, and visions of the giant paycheck you would be receiving in a few short days, was like no other feeling. On top of that the gnarliest vacation of my life was looming in the foreground of my mind the entire three days. It was a time when everything seemed just right, life was vivid and brilliant, all the pieces were in place.

Checkout in Nashville was a hectic two-day process of completing paperwork; essentially calculating and tallying all the financial and inventory records from the past three months of selling books. Having delivered a small garage full worth of books that summer, I had a hellacious time trying to get all my numbers to match up to the company's records. During the day we crunched numbers, in the evenings we partied with all the friends that we had not seen the whole summer. Students poured into Nashville from all corners of America, weary from the road and running on fumes. Some people had driven throughout the night. Others had not showered in days. It was a ragtag mix of students in various states of mental exhaustion, like marathoners struggling the last few paces to the finish.

The first night in town I finally got some private time with Heidi. I had been waiting for over four months. Patience came to fruition and we could finally touch and kiss each other. It was a relief to be able to express ourselves and talk about the feelings we had been burying for so long. During the day we were able to display our affection without having to hide. Nashville was heavenly. When all was said and done I had a check for just over $15,000 in my pocket. As there was no time to waste I quickly got back to the highway. I pointed my car north to Chicago and prepared my mind for loading all the necessary shit I would need for my trip into a giant blue backpack I had borrowed from a friend.

I only spent one day back home in the suburbs at my folks' place packing. The next two days were up in Milwaukee saying hello/goodbye to all of my people in the city, as well as spending every possible moment with the fair-skinned blondy that I was so madly in love with. I speak about her skin because the majority of our time was spent in the nude, exploring each other's bodies as fervently as Lewis & Clark did the Louisiana Purchase, minus the mapmaking. Due to her summer success she had won two round trip plane tickets anywhere in the U.S. in some contests that our manager had thrown out as incentives. Thankfully she chose to cash them in for one ticket to visit me in Europe at the end of September. I was amped about her blind commitment, flattered that she was as gaga over me as I was over her, and relieved that I would only need to wait three or four weeks to see her again.

PART 11 - THE WORLD'S GREATEST

On the morning of our departure flight, Evan and I had breakfast with my maternal grandparents, Bob and Betty. They were thrilled about our upcoming trip and wanted to see us off before my little sister Lindsay drove us to the airport. Grandma and Grandpa Sauerberg loved their grandchildren, my sisters and I, so much that they followed us a year after we moved to a new town in the Chicago suburbs. The most important thing in their life was being a part of ours. In our formative years they had played a critical role in raising us.

When I was four years old, my parents were building an addition on our family home in Palatine, Illinois. Rather than rent another home during construction we stayed with grandma and grandpa in the home where my mom had been raised. My sisters would play with toys my own mother had used in her childhood. Grandma would read us the same books. This was the most joyful time I can remember as a youngster.

Every Sunday morning Grandma would toil in the kitchen, whipping up an inordinate amount of homemade pancakes, eggs and breakfast sausage. A portly, consistently jovial lady, she took no greater pleasure than in feeding her family, making sure everyone was well served before sitting down to eat herself. Then she would lovingly insist that we take second helpings after clearing our plates. Even if you were not hungry you would have to keep eating just because it made her so happy. I have seen elderly women who drink coffee from "World's Greatest Grandma" mugs, but those ladies are lying, because my grandma was undoubtedly the best. In later years when my parents were unable to pick us kids up from school or drive to whatever sporting event or doctor's appointment we needed to attend, Grandma would be there in her shiny champagne Cadillac Deville, honking the horn embarrassingly and waving ecstatically.

Grandma and Grandpa owned two different Cadillacs in their retirement. I will never forget the day they pulled into our driveway with a monstrous dark blue schooner called the Fleetwood Brougham. We are talking about the late eighties body style with flamboyant winged tail lights and a trunk big enough to satisfy the needs of even the most industrious mafia hit man. Hearing the horn blow from inside the house, my sisters and I rushed to the window of the living room to see them sitting contently in their new boat. Most retired folks purchase big, fancy luxury cars so as to reward themselves for decades of hard work and savings. My grandparents bought their Caddy so they would have enough room and comfort for taxiing us grandkids.

Their favorite place to take us was up to the small resort town of Lake Geneva, Wisconsin. Originally a summer haven for wealthy Chicago families like the Wrigleys, Lake Geneva is the perfect weekend trip where folks of simple means can enjoy one of the few beaches in the Chicago area. Every time we made the hour-long trip north the Caddy was packed full with sandwiches, sodas, fresh fruit, towels, sunscreen, and of course our boogie boards; gifts from them for Christmas one year. Looking back, it's unbelievable to imagine how much joy they took from our simple childhood happiness. Grandpa's favorite activity was always playing "Johnny Jump Up", a silly water game that involved holding your arms and legs up in the air and counting, "One Johnny jump up… two Johnny jump up… three Johnny jump up… four Johnny jump up!" You would have to yell the last part pretty quickly. When you threw your last leg up you obviously fell straight into the water. He would be laughing hysterically when you resurfaced and wiped the water out of your eyes.

Another favorite was Great America, a sprawling amusement park thirty miles north of Chicago. Grandma would follow us kids and our friends around all day while we rode roller coasters and stuffed cotton candy in our faces. She never complained, just sat on a bench smiling and reading her book until we returned.

When my family was building our home in Prairie Grove we had the fortune of living right next door to grandma and grandpa. My great-grandparents, James and Marie, had lived in the house we inherited for over thirty years. I never got to meet my great-grandma, who passed away before I was born, but distinctly remember great-grandpa as a lovely old man. He lived to ninety-one years of age, dying from Alzheimer's when I was eight. Around the time of his death, my parents were planning the design of our new home. When great-grandpa's sickness was too severe we checked him into the nursing home and his place became vacant. We were able to sell our old home quickly so it only made sense to spend the year there.

My dad has worked in construction his whole adult life and took this project on as a personal mission. Much time was spent planning and negotiating with the architect in order to get every detail just right. The home was to be my parents' dream house. During the building process, Dad put in countless hours of work with Mom at the end of his laborious, exhausting job in the city. Everyone contributed to the project. Lauren, Lindsay, and I got on our hands and knees laying tile in the kitchen in the summer. One year I spent Christmas Eve shoveling snow off the foundation with pops. We wanted to complete as many of the jobs as possible ourselves, to build something of our own.

That year we were the happiest kids at Jane Adams Elementary School, a mere block away from our temporary home. On the first day of school not only my mom, but also Grandma and Grandpa saw us off in the morning. After school we would sprint back to their house for a snack and sometimes stay for dinner, supper, as Grandma referred to it. My parents were usually working on the house until late at night.

On the weekend and summers morning we would wake up and skip over to Grandma and

Grandpas for breakfast and tea. Grandpa would sit in his rocker chair smoking a pipe, reading the funnies (comic pages) and working on the crossword puzzle from the Chicago Tribune. Grandma prepared tea that we were allowed to drink from elaborately designed fine China that had belonged to her mother. She displayed the pristine cups and saucers proudly in a Curio cabinet in the dining room. She always spoke of her mother adoringly and reminded us that we needed to be VERY careful with these precious heirlooms. My sisters and I would set up a little blue pot full of hot tea and a dish of Domino sugar cubes to sweeten the tea to our palate's content. We acted like royalty holding our tea parties, allowing our endless childhood imaginations to run wild. We would get dressed up in fancy clothes and pretend to be wealthy socialites, sipping the finest teas with elegance and grace.

In the evenings we would all play poker; five-card draw, no peek baseball, and screw your neighbor. Grandma and Grandpa were card players and would gamble with friends placing penny to quarter-sized bets. The closet in their hallway held numerous jars full of change. Each of us kids was given our own small jar in which to keep our pennies, and would play and bet just like big people. It wasn't as risky as when I played hundred dollar hands of black jack in Vegas years later.

Nonetheless, we felt like big shots counting our haul at the end of play. It was with a tinge of sadness that we moved away that next year into our beautiful new home in a strange new town. Us grandkids were the greatest joy in their lives and they could not stay away for long.

The cozy ranch house Grandma and Grandpa moved into in Crystal Lake a year later was only three miles from our own, and a mile from my school. We held most family holidays at their place because Grandma loved hosting and cooking for us. The advantage of their proximity to our school was that when I had lunch release junior and senior years of high school, instead of driving three times further to go home, or to waste my money at McDonalds, I could visit them. Grandma prepared delicious meals not only for me but also my buddy Jon Syre, who loved talking about fishing with Grandpa. Jon was an avid fisherman and Gramps had a seemingly endless well of stories and jokes to tell him. He would always laugh along politely no matter how dry or stupid the joke. Grandma had heard all these yarns before and would reprimand Grandpa afterwards.

"Oh Bob, he doesn't want to hear that," she exclaimed in a lovingly perturbed tone.

Sometimes lunch was just macaroni and cheese or pizza, but on certain special occasions we had a juicy steak and potatoes waiting on our plates. Sitting in Calculus forth period with empty stomachs, instead of paying attention to the teacher, Jon and I would speculate, "What do you think, pizza or Mexican casserole today?"

Another way to bring us grandkids around was by finishing their basement. They purchased all the materials for my dad and me to install the framing. The carpet and drywall work was hired out. Soon we had space for two single beds, a couch, recliner, television, and heavy circular oak table with chairs cut out of full-sized rum barrels. They also bought a mini fridge to keep our soda cold and avoid having to go upstairs. I took advantage of the basement more than either of my sisters. Many weekend nights freshman and sophomore year I would invite a friend, usually Jon, to come over and play video games. We snuck any skunky old cans of beers or hard liquor we could get our hands on down to the basement and experimented with varying levels of drunkenness. One time we got a hold of some moonshine, 190 proof, that was hiding in the back of their liquor cabinet. It was a whole new level of intoxication for a fifteen year old. The next day I felt like my head was being squeezed in a vice. Another time they caught us smoking cigars. In our young minds we must have thought that because they were old they were also hard of smelling. I guess it was just youthful ignorance and a false sense of invincibility. They were pretty upset at the time, but it did not last for long.

The importance that Grandma and Grandpa played in this trip was not only in seeing us off properly on the morning of our departure, but also in helping me establish the sense of wonder about the world that inspired me to travel in the first place. Throughout my youth they were always talking about the trips they had taken to Europe with other couples from back in their old neighborhood in Chicago. Many of Grandma's proudest possessions were the trinkets picked up along the way. She spoke highly of the glorious countries they had seen, Germany, Belgium and England mostly, and how warm the people were. Since my family only took one big vacation to Disney World when we were younger, I believe a great part of my proclivity towards travel came from them. But this would certainly not be the only positive trait Grandma would bestow upon me.

Besides my own parents, no one else would influence the person I became in adulthood as much as my grandma. An extremely successful woman, she rose to the position of Vice President of Operations at the LaGrange Bank where she worked for twenty plus years. Nowadays it's rare for someone to stay at one company, specifically a bank, for more than a few years before climbing up the career ladder. At the time in the early eighties, this was no small feat for a woman. It was still rare to see a female rise to such high roles of management in the male dominated business world. She did so without a college degree, just a solid work ethic and compassion for people. Whenever I achieved accolades in school or sports, Grandma would be the first one to congratulate me. The remark she made most often was, "Wesley, I'm so proud of you."

I couldn't have asked for a more loving, supportive grandparent.

Having been successful in business herself, she was always encouraging me and assuring me that I would be successful too. It was her insistence that led me to acquire my first set of golf clubs and take lessons. She was constantly reminding me, "The golf course is where business deals are made."

I even started caddying at the local country club when I was only thirteen because of her encouragement to begin saving money and to learn as much as I could about the affluent men who played there. Grandpa had been a golfer in his healthier days too, but his eyesight got to be so bad he had to give up the game at an unfortunately early age. We did get to play together one time, a day I will always cherish.

Throughout my schooling, every honor roll certificate was applauded, every endeavor supported, and no one clapped harder at the eighth grade graduation ceremony speech I gave in the school auditorium for achieving the salutatorian status of our class of a hundred. She had tears in her eyes when I completed high school with honors and gave me a gigantic hug only a grandma could give on the day of college graduation.

"I'm so proud of you," she said yet again. "I love you so much."

As always, making sure I was well fed before my big journey, Grandma and Grandpa drove with us into town and treated Evan and me to a delicious, hearty breakfast at the fanciest joint in town. They were both so happy for us and proud of our working hard in the summer to earn this opportunity. Back at their house when we dropped them off I had my little sister Lindsay take a picture of the four of us, Evan and I with mischievous smiles, on the new digital camera I was borrowing from Heidi for the trip. Then I snapped a shot of just the two of them, lovebirds of fifty-five years. Everyone hugged goodbye, and it was off to O'Hare International Airport in my sister's red Pontiac. Little did I know this would be the last picture taken of them together.

PART III - THE
RAIL DOGS

From the moment we landed in Paris early the morning of September 4th after an overnight flight, we had just one goal: get to Amsterdam as soon as possible to purchase hydroponic marijuana legally at a coffee shop. From Charles DeGaulle, a shabby, unorganized mess of an airport, we caught a shuttle bus to the du Nord train station in the heart of the city. This task in itself took about an hour because we couldn't figure out which tickets we needed or where to wait. The weariness from the flight certainly did not help. The next train from Paris to Amsterdam, we discovered, departed in two hours. We lugged our backpacks to a café just across street to wait. I ordered a café au lait (coffee with milk) and a scone. Evan had studied French in high school and was interested in spending more time in Paris, but we figured it would be just as easy on the back end of the trip before flying home. Besides, with all the negative stories I had heard and read about what assholes the Parisians are, I was weary.

The weather was a mild seventy degrees, the morning sun just having ascended above the rooftops of the classic Parisian architecture. Both of us wore shit eating grins across our faces as we passed the time playing Gin Rummy. Sitting at a small outdoor table, drinking our cafes, playing cards and smoking cigarettes, we immediately acclimated to the easy-going, laissez-faire European lifestyle that would be our staple for the next two months. I pulled out the rail system maps acquired upon purchasing our Rail Passes. Together we mapped out a general route we hoped to follow, including stops in Prague, Czech Republic, Munich, Germany for Oktoberfest, Vienna, Austria, Budapest, Hungary, and multiple stops in Switzerland, Italy, and Spain before returning to gay old Paris. Battling the frantic morning shuffle of the train station, we boarded our first car of the trip and rolled off to the many guilty pleasures of Amsterdam.

On the train we scribbled excitedly in our journals and listened to CDs on our Discmen, barreling through the Belgian countryside in a rickety train car. Evan fell asleep listening to Radiohead while I sampled the new three disc "Dick's Picks" Grateful Dead set. It would prove itself invaluable whilst riding the rails and living as a transient for the weeks to come. I kept thinking that Evan was a natural for this type of lifestyle. The way he slouched back on his seat with a calm smirk across his face, legs crossed ankle over knee, his pen contemplatively stroking the pages of paper in front of him. I knew I had chosen the perfect companion.

The first order of business upon arrival in Amsterdam was to find a place to stay. The sooner this happened the sooner we could drop off our cumbersome packs and find a sufficient coffee shop. The sky was clear and blue, the air fresh and crispy, and the trees wore the bright red, orange and yellow hues of autumn. The city bustled with life, but in some way the air felt like it lacked tension. It was as if these people were carrying themselves with the knowledge of historic experience. We walked through a diverse afternoon crowd of commuters, tourists, street performers, police, and shopkeepers.

On a street called the Haarlemmerstraat, our search for a hostel came to an end. A friendly Jewish girl named Nolya, a few years our senior, asked us if we were looking for lodging. We were amazed at this great fortune without even considering how obviously we must have stood out with our full packs and wandering eyes. Nolya walked us, alongside her bicycle, the preferred method of transportation in the city, to a first floor laundry mat. Here we met two friendly men we guessed were Indian, who said we could stay in an upstairs apartment for just twenty Euros apiece. The room contained ample space, a kitchen, two beds, a table and chairs, and French windows with a third story view of all the action taking place on the straat below. We dropped our packs, powdered our noses, and headed out to fill our empty bellys.

Over the course of a few days in Amsterdam these men became like family. More specifically, the Indian man became like our dad, and the other, a Sri Lankan with a full black beard, became like our dirty uncle. Anytime we sought advice from the two, our adopted father would refer us to hip, trendy restaurants, bargain souvenir shops, and popular tourist attractions. Our uncle, on the other hand, was more apt to send us to the appropriate spots to find good drugs and sex for a reasonable price. Both gentlemen would prove invaluable in the course of our four-night stay. They were very difficult to leave in the end.

After settling in and grabbing showers we went for a walk. We stopped at an empty pizza joint and ordered up a couple of slices of marguerite; a plain cheese pizza with oregano, and Heinekens. After a full twenty-four hour commute to the liberal, freethinking, legislatively lenient capital of The Netherlands, these cold domestic beers were perfectly soothing to our dehydrated throats.

"Welp," said the casual Quackenbush, "I'm glad we followed through on this thing."

All I could do was laugh and clink his Heineken with mine, on the bottom of course, since Evan and I only bottom clink our drinks. We even have our own private drinking club called the Bottom Clinkers with numerous honorary members, but I digress.

The curly, greasy black haired young dude who served us had an inordinate amount of energy. He was bouncing to and fro in rhythm with the rapid, intricate techno beats that blared from two large stadium sized speakers behind the counter. Due to his inexplicable display of gusto so early on a Friday afternoon, we dubbed him "coked out pizza guy". Already feeling enriched by the fascinating new people we were meeting, and highly motivated to begin exploring the local scene, we bid farewell to the one-man rave at the pizza parlor and headed to the streets.

After no more than two blocks we bumped into The Rokerij, a dark, gothic coffee shop situated alongside a canal. Our good friend T.J., who had traveled here while he was studying in Florence, Italy, had recommended it.

"How fortuitous," we thought.

The outside patio in front included a couple of tables accompanied with unusual, stumpy chairs carved out of giant logs of wood. The overall appearance was black and mystical. Upon entering, we spotted two long benches running the length of the walls on either side with thick cushioned seats, ottomans and small tables. Each table held one individual white candle burning solemnly. To the right, just past the entrance, was a dark, clandestine booth in which a mysterious bohemian man with large ear hole piercings and tattoos was seated behind a small window. On the counter sat a price list that detailed over a dozen different strains of cannabis as well as a handful of hashish varieties.

Neither of us had any experience with hash, a purified cannabis resin in block or chewy form, so we focused intently on the weed. Each variety was sold in 1-gram packages, labeled neatly with a type written sticker. As I was clearly too overwhelmed and awestruck to decide between all the options, White Widow,

Kalamist, Bubblegum, Blueberry; Evan took advantage of the opportunity to step up and purchase. He opted for the Bubblegum strain, handed the well-concealed man a ten Euro bill, and turned around with an ear-to-ear grin like he had just been released from prison. While still completely discombobulated by the ability to purchase marijuana in public, I followed Evan's cool display by very nervously ordering the exact same thing. Instead of taking the opportunity to sample another variety, and mix things up a bit, I folded under the pressure. Immediately castigating myself for such a foolish decision, my remorse drifted away with the smoke of our first stiff joint.

In Europe, marijuana smokers generally mix their pot with tobacco to reduce the strength of the joint, conserve the drug, and most importantly increase the incendiary capacity of the spliff; the nickname for such cigarette. Sticky, potent marijuana will not burn as cleanly and naturally as tobacco will, henceforth producing runs up the side of the paper, or just simply burning out. However, as Americans fully accustomed to consuming all things in excess, we held steadfastly to the custom of rolling pure joints with 100% pot.

We had ever smoked anything in the same ballpark as this weed, and after one joint were seriously blazed. Not to mention that the papers we were using were twice the normal

size of a cigarette paper back home. We sat
back reclined on the benches for the next
hour staring across the aisle at the regu-
lars rolling up and smoking their joints in
a relaxed, easy manner. They sat quietly and
calmly, many people by themselves, and gazed
off into the distance, existing in their own
personal worlds. There was very little conversation. We opted to make our way down the
road before too long to avoid the smoky haze
in which the others were living. For us, pot
was a social drug, used to induce laughter,
conversation, and hilarity. From this point
on, there would be little time spent in this
city in which we were not in a similar state
of mind, comfortably stoned.

The following stop just a few doors down
along the canal was a bar named "Old Style",
after the Milwaukee brewed beer that was so
commonly available back home. The name excited
me because my father has been a hardcore
Old Style Man his whole life, rarely holding another beer up to his lips. Evan is a
huge fan on account of nostalgic reasons.
This was the first legal beer we had together
on my twenty-first birthday. The bar served
alcohol, not cannabis, but our cottony mouths
were in need of moisture. So Evan approached
the bartender and asked him politely for two
Old Styles. The amiable dreadlocked gentleman
behind the bar kind of gritted his teeth and

offered only an apologetic half-smile exclaiming in a heavy Dutch accent that, "we do not serve it here."

He then painfully added, "I hear it is a horrible beer."

We ordered up some Stella Artois' instead and sat down at a side table scratching our heads, reviewing the brief conversation to try to make sense of this place. It took us about five minutes to come to our senses. We realized that we cared not to endorse a bar that operated under such false pretenses.

"A horrible beer," we scoffed, and strolled out the front door.

An outstanding feature of the city of Amsterdam, apart from the canal network that divides the city like a sheet of graphing paper, is the amount of bicycles. Because the roadways are so narrow, having been constructed of cobblestone in the seventeenth century, and the cost of gasoline so expensive, bicycling is the preferred mode of transportation for everyone from young adults all the way up to the elderly. Prior to the trip, I viewed bicycle riding as a sport only for active enthusiasts and children. I have an enduring image of the line of bicycles chained up at the train station on the north end of the city where we arrived. It consisted of four ascending stories and ramps with, in my best possible estimation, about five hundred bikes locked up to posts on each level. It was absolutely astounding.

Upon returning to the Haarlemmerstraat, leaving unsatisfied from the "Old Style", we saw two elderly folks turning the corner on their bicycles. Suddenly, in the slow motion haze of my first joint at the Rokerij, I watched the woman very gradually tumble to the ground like an ape being shot from a tree with a tranquilizer dart. As she fell she uttered a meek, surprised "Oooh," and then crashed to the pavement.

Evan reacted more quickly than I by rushing to her aid and assisting the older gentleman in hoisting his disheveled wife from the street. She simply brushed herself off, smiled and nodded her thanks towards the Norwegian. Then they were off on their way again. No one else on the road seemed to pay any mind, but we continued laughing hysterically as we strolled happily towards the next coffee shop. It's not every day that you see a seventy-year-old woman bail on a bicycle in the middle of a bustling city street. Especially not while on weed.

At this time I would like to expound upon the wondrous treasures, tramps and troubadours we saw on our beloved Haarlemmerstraat. The first of these was the Pablow Picasso coffee shop located adjacent to our home above the laundry mat. The interior of said shop consists of a two-story lofted café with a mixture of Picasso's cubist and surrealist period prints on the walls. The sign on the front window advertises a free breakfast from 8:30 to 11:00am. Naturally we gravitated to the impossibly convenient free grub to find out that, as always in life there was a "catch". The catch being that the gratuitous meal was offered in condition with a minimum purchase of 5 grams of hash or marijuana. Since we were already planning on buying hash that day, the offer was irresistible.

Hash can be smoked in many different ways, but the easiest for us was to roll it up in our cigarettes. First you have to melt the product with a lighter until it becomes soft and pliable. I selected a nice gooey chunk of Barassa, while Evan chose a denser, hard packed Turkish version. Once it's sufficiently heated, you roll it between your fingers like clay until it morphs into a long, thin snake-like string that can be placed upon tobacco and rolled accordingly. The affects of hash are a bit different than marijuana. We felt a greater tingling sensation in our bodies and were less giggly. The meal was a proper English breakfast with eggs, muffins, jam, bacon, coffee, juice, fruit salad, and a bubblegum joint. I can say with confidence that there is no finer manner in which to begin your day on the Haarlemmerstraat.

Another charm of our street was the random roller-skating parade which whizzed past our eyes at about 9pm our first evening in town. Walking unassumingly down the tranquil straat the first night, a sudden commotion up the way grabbed our attention. It was a procession of a few hundred people of all ages speeding past on roller-skates and rollerblades, adorned with glow sticks and bright red lights flashing on their wheels and clothing. It was one constant stream of banners, idiotic smiles and chanting, for about three full minutes. The people in the procession were having the absolute time of their lives. We looked at each other in amazement. "Wow. That was quite a spectacle," said Evan.

Afterwards the street returned to its quiet, solemn self.

The final, and undoubtedly finest feature of the Haarlemmerstraat, was direct access to the techno party that blared down below our window when we awoke on Sunday morning. From the third floor we saw a DJ with turntables set up just in front our beloved Pablow Picasso, mixing up delectable house beats for "break"fast. Techno was all the rage in Europe at the time. More than just music, the street was full of merchants with display carts pedaling everything from gimcracks and folderols, to produce and home furnishings. After briefly feigning interest in their wares we gravitated back to the action of the techno party, which had since escalated into a full-scale street jam.

A few beers and hash joints later, we were really getting into the whole production. The primary party goers were a few middle-aged men in blue jeans and denim jackets, an Indian man, not from India, but a native American Indian with a long black ponytail, the DJ, a transient gypsy woman, and a scamp of a Jackrussel terrier. We called him Eddy, because he looked like an Eddy, but later learned his name was Boy. The weather was cloudy and overcast with intermittent drizzle, but failed to diminish the enjoyment of the participants. It was enough to see the middle-aged men bobbing up and down in their state of drunkenness with no rhythm, but the Indian cat was actually emceeing the show with a portable microphone. Everyone was kicking a plastic bottle around while Eddy chased it eagerly.

Meanwhile, in between the ominous rain clouds, locals continued on about their weekend business totally uninterrupted. Some of the younger, more tolerant passersby would stop for a moment to observe, or simply groove to the music while they walked or rode by on bicycles. One elderly couple of tourists really got into the show by stopping to dance. A few snobby yuppies seemed disgusted by the trampy street folk, such as ourselves, and tried to ignore us as they walked by in knit sweaters with their noses in the air. When nobody got out of their way they reacted even more haughtily. The highlight of the show was undoubtedly the grand finale in which the already shirtless Indian dude, commentating with mic in hand, dropped his jeans to the ground and began jumping up and down completely nude. Everyone carried on unaffected while Evan and I fell to the sidewalk in laughter.

"Haarlemmerstraat is in the house," he exclaimed bombastically, "Everybody's in the house." We could not have agreed more. Nor could we stop repeating those two phrases for the rest of the trip. We even ended up getting to meet the emcee later in evening at "The Doors" coffee shop. It was our closest brush with fame while in Holland.

After witnessing the flyby Friday night roller skating festival, we made our way to Boom Chicago, an improv comedy club recommended by our new father, the sagacious travel counselor. The shows were in English and included a mostly American cast. The humor was sub-par, and one of the girls got snotty with me from stage when I made a sarcastic comment out loud that was actually more comical than her act. We hung out with a few of the players after the set and got properly pissed on giant glasses of beer. The real humor occurred later when Evan and I attempted to drunkenly navigate our way back to the Haarlemmerstraat based on pure instinct alone, and got lost. We had gotten a ride in a small Peugeot hatchback from some cool British guys we met at the club, but somehow ended up in an eerily quiet residential neighborhood.

We then found an old bicycle with a flat tire resting up against a tree that had been spray-painted bright neon green. It was in the classic 1970's fashion with the high rounded handlebars and banana seat. Although I am usually not prone to thievery, I just could not resist. I jumped on the seat, and when Evan attempted to join me, my legs gave out and we toppled directly onto the cobblestone sidewalk. Not much unlike the old lady earlier in the day, actually. For sheer entertainment value, and because I was too drunk to be discerning, I rode the bicycle full speed towards a canal, jumping off just in time to watch it soar into the water. The ghostrider. We ran away speedily and hysterically. I am sure that bad things have happened to me since, karmic reparations if you will. We carried on for another hour unable to reconcile our geographic position to the map. Finally, we met a Finnish guy on the street named Hans who helped us relocate our beloved Haarlemmerstraat.

Located across from a central building known as the "Old Church", the Red Light District originally developed as a series of "houses of pleasure", or luxury brothels where sailors and soldiers could enjoy music, dance, and the company of prostitutes. On the second night we sought guilty pleasures, or at least exposure to others partaking in such pleasures. On our lascivious new uncle's advice, we paid a visit to the infamous district. The neighborhood is named for the bright fluorescent lights that frame the hundreds of display windows facing the streets. Behind these sit scantily clad women attempting to lure desperate, horny, and lonely men into their chambers for some good old-fashioned copulation. A liberal port city, Amsterdam is world renowned for its legal acceptance of prostitution and drug use. Passing the many sex shops, live sex shows, cannabis and sex museums, and generally seedy-looking individuals, we knew we were in the right place.

Once inside the district, we probably didn't go two minutes without having the words "ecstasy" or "coke" inquisitively whispered into our ears by strangers looking to profit off of curious tourists. Disinterested in hard drugs, we sauntered on pretending not to hear their passive-aggressive propositions. We had plenty of hash and pot to last us for the first month of the trip, didn't want to spend $40 on a live sex show, and had no interest in filthy intercourse, I mean coitus. Instead we created our own little game to entertain ourselves.

It was called "Wave at the Hookers."

It doesn't take much imagination to figure out the rules of this game. All you have to do is make eye contact with any of the countless provocative women of the night standing in the pink or red glow of the neon tube lights. When they begin seducing you with their eyes, offer a sincere, honest smile and wave back and forth with reckless abandon like a child saying goodbye to their mom at the bus stop on the first day of Kindergarten. One of two things will then happen. Either you will receive the same gleeful smile and wave in kind, or a snarled, pissed off death stare that elucidates their contempt for your condescension. Either way, it's buckets of fun and really brightens up the evening. We continued exploring until we got bored and called it a night.

Above and beyond, our favorite spot to pass time in Amsterdam was the Vanderpark. The charm of Vanderpark, or Mushroom Park, as the locals call it (more on that later), was the ability to share pristine park space with a cornucopia of people in a wide variety of psychological and mental states. On our first visit we just threw our Frisbee in the shade of two immense oak trees adjacent to a small pond in the middle of the park. At one point we stopped due to a commotion caused by one of the aforementioned park denizens that was attacking another man with his arms and fists flailing wildly, screaming in a British accent, "Don't touch my fucking dog. Don't you ever touch my fuuuuuuuuuucking dawwwg!"

We had missed the prelude to this part of the story and could only assume that the innocent man had touched the lunatic's fucking dog. Seemingly harmless, we thought, but this disheveled hobo was bloody well angry.

After the park we checked out the Van Gogh Museum, a short walk up the street. Here lives the world's largest, most impressive display of the one-eared Dutch painter and his contemporaries' impressionist collections. Although we would most aptly be described as art novices, we both thoroughly enjoyed the museum. Van Gogh had the ability to turn the most basic landscape, a vase of flowers, or even a person's face into a fully earthy, organic scene. His use of colors left me feeling warm and the waves of finger strokes on the canvas emanated a sense of beauty in their simplicity. The museum itself, consisting of two buildings, holds its own independent aesthetic. The exterior is a slate gray hue. One building is a half circle with curvy Nuevo modern lines and has a shallow pool in front. The other rectangular portion features sharp, square lines, and two industrial window façades on one of its corners. The interior space, vast and open, has clean, simplistic white walls and blond hardwood flooring. The contemporary design is an ironic juxtaposition to the nineteenth-century art on display, yet its meshing of styles leaves the visitor awash in the beauty of both periods.

Furthermore, we enjoyed the immense flat, green public space outside the museum used by the transient youth of Amsterdam for skateboarding, practicing marching band numbers, and taking naps. From a hill at the opposite end of the field we continued to take in the museum's splendor from afar. After bathing in the afternoon sun for a couple of hours in the commons, we stopped to watch some old men playing chess on a life size board on the pavement in the middle of a shopping center by the park. The pieces were about two feet tall and the public match had attracted a significant crowd of spectators. One competitor, an elderly man with gray hair wearing a Babushka, who maybe stood four feet high, could be heard uttering unintelligible words and grunting under his breath. The other man eyed the board intently, ignoring the showmanship of his opponent.

"Rook, pawn, mumble, and grumble," were the gist of the small old man's excitations. In the end his nonsensical machinations were too much to compete with. The crowd broke into a delighted applause at the call of "checkmate." We continued walking through the city with our enlightened eyes wandering enthusiastically for the next sight that would grab our attention.

Our next experience at Vanderpark involved hallucinogenic mushrooms. It was actually our

second time purchasing these healthy vegetables. We didn't realize the first time that
they were not like the dried Mexican version
found in the States. These were the fresh,
refrigerated version that spoil and turn black
if not eaten shortly after purchase.

"Can we still eat these?" we asked the
clerk who sold them to us, holding a blatantly
rancid bag of fungus up in the air.

"No, they will make you very sick."

Ok, dodged a bullet on that one. Walking
into the park after picking up our second
batch, an Ecuadorian sample that was listed
as the second most powerful in the world, we
were giddy like schoolgirls in anticipation
for what was about to go down.

I turned to Evan and said, "I can't wait
to see what these things are gonna make me
want to do."

Little did I know that sitting on a bench
staring at a concrete statue of a fish for
four hours was what they would make me do.
Munching down our psychedelic snack under a
tree, washing them down forcefully with lots
of water, we filled our bellies with the hearty,
less than tasty stems and caps.

Next we made our way over to the bench
and waited expectantly for crazy time. Evan
spotted a couple of cute, young blond moms
who were escorting a small group of youngins
around the park. They were in the middle of

knocking acorns down from a tree with sticks, chuckling and jumping up and down with glee. He quickly seized the opportunity to join in the fun. Just as Evan began dancing around with the ladies and children, I fell victim to a pretty serious case of the giggles. When he returned to the bench he handed me a large shiny brown nut, which I would hold onto for dear life for the rest of my trip. Then he dropped a handful of nuts into our Frisbee with a mischievous smirk on his countenance and began tossing them up in the air and catching them in the disc. I knew for sure at this point that they had hit me. We continued to talk to one another in between fits of laughter that would leave me short of breath with an aching belly. In the beginning the sensation was very intense and I felt as if I might be sick to my stomach. After about a half an hour this subsided and I was on my way to the moon.

Suddenly Quack was off wandering around, examining the many marvels that a public park has to offer a man ripped to his tits on Psilocybin. I opted for lying on my bench, clutching my magic nut tightly, staring up at the somber gray clouds that were pulsating and booming, and the bold green treetops swirling and shimmering like a thousand mountain streams.

"As the French would say, I'm having some major cloud visuals," I exclaimed to no one.

At one point a small dog meandered past my bench, and I called him Eddy. In fact, I called every dog Eddy; it was just easier that way. He wasn't exactly speaking to me as he scampered by, stopping briefly to sniff the invalid gazing upside down at him from the bench, but I definitely felt an unspoken spiritual connection with this canine. We had become cosmic equals on a supernatural playing field.

The running/biking path in front of the bench offered plenty of entertainment. One guy was slowly, peacefully biking past sweetly singing the song "Creep" by Radiohead. We had just heard a man playing it in a doorway on the street with his acoustic guitar the night before. Creepy. A fashionable older man dressed in a black silk suit with a white panama hat, most likely a secret agent, gave me a curious glance as he passed. Another young guy rode past on a long skateboard swaying back and forth with a smooth, rhythmic fluidity that reminded me of the Nintendo game "Paperboy." It felt like he probably circled around seven or eight times, but counting was certainly out of the realm of my capabilities by now. In fact, a majority of the time I just nestled myself into the fetal position, smiling, laughing, and doing my best not to fall off of the face of the planet. The fish statue was not about to make that an easy task, taunting me with its puckered lips, and fancy, intricate scales.

Eventually, after what seemed to be about three lifetimes and a day, Evan returned to share in my whimsy. We gradually made our way down the emotional curve of the mushroom trip.

"You know Evan, when you're on mushrooms, you feel like you are never going to be off mushrooms again… EVER."

"I know," he confirmed gravely.

He informed me that he had been off enjoying spontaneous mental impulses, climbing trees, and visualizing all sorts of madness. He had just finished writing in his journal and talking to a local woman and her son. With her help he was able to convince the innocent boy he was a famous writer from America.

Walking through the park we ran into a couple of Rastafarian guys that were playing a tambourine and a berimbau, a single stringed instrument attached to a large gourd with a long bent stick, played in the Brazilian martial art dance of Capoeira. We broke into an impromptu mushroom jig that put a knowing smile on their faces. Easing our way back into reality we then found a café and took a spot of coffee and some cookies. We spent some time delving into a deep conversation about all the places our minds had ventured throughout the trip. Afterwards we walked away singing "What's Goin On?" by the 4 Non Blondes (the song was playing at the café) at the top of our lungs in the shrillest female voice possible, stopping briefly to compose ourselves from laughter attacks. Finally, we celebrated the commencement of our long journey with a carafe of wine and some Greek cuisine in town. At dinner we chatted with a kooky middle-aged British travel agent who was dining next to us with her third husband. In her earlier days, she explained cheekily, she had been "bad, very, very bad."

The entire day had been a trip within a trip.

The next day we had a lazy morning, enjoying another free breakfast at Pablow Picasso's before meandering around town. We both felt lazy after coming down off the intense endorphin rush of the prior day. Things were a touch cloudy when we walked into a random coffee shop to have a beer and play some pool. To our surprise the bartender prohibited us from carrying our plastic Nalgene bottle full of water inside. He was perfectly happy with us rolling up our own marijuana and smoking it in his establishment, but H_2O was strictly off limits. Our confusion continued when we played a game of pool with another customer and his girlfriend. At the end of the game she scratched on the 8 Ball, missing her shot and sending the cue ball into one of the pockets. We assumed we had won and were getting ready to re-rack when they stopped us.

"You scratched, so we win the game," I said matter of factly.

"No, we do not play that rule," said the man.

"Alright," I thought, taking my next shot and sinking the 8 Ball clean, ostensibly winning the game. I walked towards them to shake hands like a good sport when he stopped me again. He explained that I needed to make the 8 Ball in the opposite pocket from where the last ball had fallen to win. Evan and I looked at each other inquisitively, clearly out of our element. We realized then that simple assumptions about the culture in each new country would be ill-advised.

One wrong assumption we made was that the majority of Dutch people would be hippy types, due of course to their lax policies on drugs and prostitution. Surprisingly most of the locals were upright, formal and conservative. The bars outside the touristy areas were flooded with preppy looking bourgeois yuppies with leather boat shoes, sweaters tied around their necks, and smart khakis. Loads of long blond-haired, sporty young men with popped collars mingled with primped, preppy blond girls with blue eyes. It was fun to have my expectations turned upside down so quickly. I knew this was going be a learning process on so many levels of which I was previously unaware.

Amsterdam was a perfect place to begin our trip and ease into the European foray. Unfortunately five days were not enough for us to see all the sights. Spending so much time in coffee shops probably did not help our cause. Most notably we missed the Anne Frank house, the secret attic dwelling of the infamous young Jewish girl whose diary from the Nazi occupation we had read in junior high school. We also failed to catch the Heineken brewery tour. It's not that we didn't have the time; we just didn't make the time. At our defense, the brewery tour was at 11am, on the other side of town, and most days we were not stumbling out of our cozy neighborhood until well after lunchtime.

The last day we explored the city at length; its long, sinuous canals and clean, well-preserved cobblestone streets. We saw many tourists taking boat tours of the city, thereby creating another game called, "Wave Condescendingly At The Tourists." The ubiquitous house barges docked throughout the canal were intriguing but we were unable to find anyone to invite us on board. By the end of

the day we felt like we had seen the city
properly. Although we could have easily spent
another five days bumming around town in a
drug induced state, it was time to head south
and drink cheap beer in Prague.

The thrill of Amsterdam continued up until
the very last moments. Deciding to take a 10pm
train ride throughout the night, thus saving a
days travel on our Rail Pass, we sadly left our
home on the Haarlemmerstraat, tearfully hugging our dad and crazy uncle goodbye. Things
would not be the same without these guardian
angles watching over us. We had to muster
up the fortitude to forge on without them.
Running short on time at the train station,
probably because we had to get high first,
I rushed through the payment line, the turn
style, and onto a car destined for Frankfurt,
Germany for an overnight transfer. I did not
immediately realize that I had boarded without
my partner in crime, who had not purchased
his ticket expediently enough. I did, however,
have his daypack with all his music, reading
material, food, and water. Suddenly, I was off
into the heart of the European continent by
my lonesome self, some four thousand miles
away from home, towards the former Soviet
Eastern Bloc.
    The unexpected sensation of loneliness was
made evermore uncomfortable by the unruly gang

of soccer hooligans en route to Germany, not for the sake of cultural enlightenment, but to get pissed drunk and rowdy whilst supporting Scotland's upcoming football (soccer) match. Despite the commotion, I was ultimately able to nod off to sleep after a tiresome, emotional week, thanks to the melodic macabre of Radiohead. My brief slumber was interrupted by the group of twenty or so young Scots chanting, laughing, and singing with drunken joy. They carried on with the raucous camaraderie for the next four hours. Meanwhile I drifted in and out of a cloudy, restless consciousness mixed with intermittent recognition of football cheers.

At one point in the middle of the night, one of the hooligans became melancholic in his stupor (drinking to excess is not merely accepted, more so encouraged in football circles), and wanted out of the escapade. His buddy pulled him aside to console him, offering these comforting words in a filthy Highlands accent, "We came ear tah do tree tings: get pist, watch sum footy, and ave a gute time, now what's wrong wit dat?"

I was slightly perturbed about not being able to sleep, but I had to admit that this bloke raised a strong argument; their plan was foolproof. I could not be too agitated by these young gents, if I were in their shoes I would certainly be carrying on in the same way. Changing trains in Frankfurt in the middle of the night, I sat next to a poor Czech lady who was wincing with back pain, having traveled to Germany for treatment. She spoke a little English and was pleasant, but had a horrendous hacking cough and moaning snore that kept me from any semblance of rest. I listened to music until falling back asleep, but was soon startled awake by the Customs Officer who needed to check my passport.

Arriving in Prague, as the sky became light once again, I felt tired and haggard. The sky was predominantly gray and cloudy. I had not slept much due to my noisy co-passengers and was missing my trusted companion. Out of sheer laziness I chose to stay in the hostel directly above the train station. It was not rated altogether highly in the *Let's Go Europe* travel book I was carrying for assistance. Throughout the course of the trip I was very glad to have brought along this indispensable traveler's companion. The thick, heavy guide gave a nice summary of the history and culture of each country, as well as anecdotes about the nuances of each specific city. Its greatest value was definitely in the broad overall summary of the continent, offering a taste of the smorgasbord in which the individual reader could choose from.

I found the specific restaurant and hostel recommendations to be average at best.

Many times I disagreed with the opinions in the book and realized that its rating system was probably based more on kickbacks to the publisher than by the actual quality of the establishments. Besides, I thought it was a waste of time to try and run around looking for specific recommendations scattered throughout a vast city rather than just exploring in the areas where I happened to be at any given time. For me the joy comes from navigating and familiarizing by feel instead of taking someone else's experience as the truth. To force the course of the journey is often less pleasurable for me than just trusting spontaneity.

The city of Prague, while vibrant and architecturally complex, can be rather dark. Having only stepped out from under the foothold of communism a decade and a half earlier, the faces of the people were comparatively colder and less inviting than Western Europe. Despondence seemed to linger in the air. I noticed that the people helping me at the post office and the restaurants were more to the point and not quite as concerned about coming across friendly. Alas, I went out on my own to explore the ancient streets and circuitous alleyways. I felt much better later that day after purchasing a slick brown knit wool Calvin Klein sweater for only twenty bucks. I celebrated by enjoying a coffee in the stunning old town square surrounded by two grand gothic churches and the Old Town Hall. The dreariness in the air somehow became comforting over time. Also, the endless line of thin, beautiful girls passing by on the streets with slender hourglass figures and large breasts enhanced my spirits. Their distinguished facial features appeared chiseled out of concrete, the way they walked with such purpose and direction was awe inspiring.

That evening I gained an awareness of just how fanatical the rest of the world is about football. Sitting at an outside dinner table on the edge of the town square at an Italian restaurant, I was surrounded by Dutch fans that had apparently followed me from the Netherlands. They were partying in preparation for the game the next day in which they would eventually lose to the Czech Republic. Dressed from head to toe in the bright orange of the national team's jerseys, some wearing orange wigs, others waving flags, all were getting schnockered on the staple Czech pilsner beer. The inexpensive, high quality brew is one of the biggest reasons so many Western Europeans vacation in Prague. Also the surprisingly well-kept architecture of the formerly Soviet-occupied territory. I ate a hearty Spaghetti Bolognese while listening to the hoots, hollers, and horns from the football crowd. One dude was banging on a huge bass drum with a mallet as the others howled along. It wasn't even the day of the game yet; this was only a warm up. It struck me as totally outrageous.

The next day I received some devastating news from back home. My Mom's best friend Jan's daughter, whom I had known as a child growing up, had been killed in an automobile accident. She was only a month into her freshman year of college at the University of Iowa. The driver was another student in an SUV whose eyes were blinded by the sun as he turned at a four-way crossing in town. His Chevy Blazer struck her in the crosswalk as she walked to her late morning class, dragging her body across the intersection. This day was the worst of my trip. I felt sad and regretful for my family and friends back home, and altogether lousy just on account of the cloudy weather. My mood was somber and lugubrious.

That evening I was sitting at a dodgy internet cafe/arcade/slot machine casino by the train station, trying to update a few friends back home of my journey, when an ugly, drunken, middle aged woman with missing teeth started harassing me. She bumped into me, spilling beer all over while trying to nudge her way into my seat. I was pushing her away forcefully, feeling aggressive myself after drinking a 16% Budvar beer with dinner, and not at all in the mood to tangle. Somewhere in the commotion my wallet fell out of my pocket. I did not notice until after I had left the cafe. When I returned ten minutes later, nervous as hell, I found the wallet with the five-Euro note still inside, but not three hundred dollars in traveler's checks. Shaken and upset, I called home and spoke with my dad. I realized there was nothing he could do for me, but he did help calm my nerves. I was able to take care of the checks the next day, yet the whole scenario left me bitter.

I learned in Prague that when you embark on life changing journeys, your experiences include incredible, ethereal highs, but also devastating, heart wrenching lows. Our planet offers beauty beyond comprehension, unimaginable joys and love in abundance, but to every up there is a down. We are fickle human beings, susceptible to the broad spectrum of emotions. No path is without its bumps and potholes.

This specific challenge taught me to accept the down times, and not get too overwhelmed. Problems will occur no matter where you are in the world or what company you keep at any given time. The key is to remind yourself that all thoughts and feelings will eventually pass. Sometimes it takes being completely isolated from all that is familiar and comfortable to learn about ourselves. We see who we are on the inside, what me are made of and how we handle adversity. At this point in time I was feeling homesick and helpless, but I focused on the only thing I could control, my attitude about my situation. I chose to lay low for the next day, knowing my trusty cohort would soon return to my side and the sun would once again break through the clouds.

In the morning I received an email from Evan stating that he was at a hostel in town with another American guy named Andy, from Oklahoma, whom he had met on the train from Amsterdam. Andy would prove to be a valuable asset, having much more experience in travel and life in general, being seven years older than us. He was about to begin graduate studies in Lancaster, England, and was taking advantage of some free time beforehand. Andy was an easygoing, slow talking Southern guy. He was intelligent and open minded, respectful and optimistic. With sarcastic wit and a penchant for absurdity, he was a perfect match for our squad. We continued on with him in Budapest, Hungary, and Oktoberfest in Munich, Germany. Getting back in touch with Evan and meeting Andy helped snap me out of my slump. My mood lightened and good times ensued.

I waited for the guys to pack up their things and then we tried our hands at Goulash for lunch. Despite the dreary, haunting name, it was actually delicious. A traditional Hungarian dish of boiled beef served with heaps of gravy, vegetables and bread, it really stuck to the ribs. The price was right, only three dollars. Having a sincere conversation at lunch, Andy shared candidly about his life and experience with love. He was unsatisfied at his job and had just broken up with a serious girlfriend. Along with his natural itch for travel, his urge to try and find his true passion was why he had decided to leave home and go back to school. Seems that following our passions can be difficult as time goes by and we settle in many areas, or simply get caught up in our lives and its responsibilities.

It became clear to me that the other travelers I met along the way would shape my trip more than anything else. Each individual human connection would alter the fate of our journey; change the outcome of our movie. Whether for the positive or negative, the people we met were going to form our strongest memories. Our minds and outlook on life post voyage would be altered much more significantly by the personalities we encountered than the marvel filled museums, monuments, or historical relics. Andy was one of the people who left an indelible mark.

The general mentality in the hostels we stayed was unlike any other I had known before.

In most situations meeting fellow backpackers such as Andy, it was incredibly comfortable and easy. Erstwhile pretensions and social inhibitions were nonexistent. Back in Tulsa, if we bumped into him at a bar, he would be a very different person, conditioned by his environment; acting in accordance with whatever adaptations he had developed in his specific social ecosystem. Meeting on neutral territory, however, people are free to let their thoughts go, to share inner fears and dreams. This is such a pure, beautiful way to be. I took great satisfaction and found refreshment in the intimate, real conversations I was able to have with fellow journeymen. It was as if the experience of human relation was so much more powerful and significant. Reason number 408 why I love to travel.

Considering the recent hullabaloo about football, we decided to go to an Irish pub to watch England playing the tiny speck on the map known as Liechtenstein. None of us are keen followers of the sport, but since it was the only one being televised, we did our best to enjoy the sacred tradition of inter-European play. We needed a sports fix and baseball was not available. Evan and I struggled with this fact because the Chicago Cubs, our favorite team, were advancing steadily in the playoffs. They were favored to reach the World Series for the first time in over fifty years. Evan was already talking about cutting the trip short to watch the series back home if they advanced. As fate would have it, an unlucky Cubs fan named Steve Bartman would disrupt this progress by knocking a foul ball out of Moises Alou's glove, thereby reversing the momentum of the entire National League Championship series. To this day, this poor soul is still blamed for single-handedly destroying the dreams of millions of Cubs fans.

At the pub we met two British lads named Paul and Chris, who were also backpacking Europe. They had fantastic stories to share about their travels. One destination they mentioned, which we would never even have considered, was Russia. They had seen Moscow and St. Petersburg. I have never really thought of Russia as being part of Europe, since its so far away, but our Rail Passes could haven taken us there. I realized we would only be scratching the very surface of possibility on this continent.

When our new mates were properly pissed up, they left the pub to hit up the titty bars in town. Instead, we walked back to the discos, not wanting to waste our hard-earned money watching boobies. Walking through the Old Town Square, we found an enormous screen erected for the locals to watch The Czech Republic play its match against The Netherlands. The square was a mess of empty bottles, food wrappers, and paraphernalia. Most of the crowd had already cleared out. We were able to procure a small Czech flag that we used to wave in the faces of the dejected Dutch supporters in the streets.

The rest of the night was spent club hopping alongside the Charles River, dancing with reckless abandon in celebration of our reunion. The clubs were nearly empty but that did not dampen the mood. We sampled Absinthe, an anise flavored, aqua colored spirit renowned as a supposedly addictive, psychoactive liquor. It was banned throughout The United States and most of Western Europe in the early twentieth century. Either we had maxed out our hallucinogenic capabilities in Amsterdam, or the potion we drank was not very potent, because neither of us experienced anything along those lines. The next day Evan and Andy moved into a large shared room at my digs above the train station, and life was good.

The zenith of our Prague experience took place the next day. Walking out of a head shop, where tobacco, posters, clothing, incense and smoking devices are readily available, Evan and I met a short, curly brown haired, goateed Californian dude named Lucas. He could not have stood more than 5'3", but what he lacked in stature he compensated for with charisma. Not five minutes after introducing ourselves, we were up on the balcony of his residence, the "Green Door", smoking pot from a small green plastic tube; otherwise known as a bong. This was more of a traveling tube than a bong though, so I will stick with the former description. From northern Cali, young Lucas possessed a bounty of fascinating stories. He could also freestyle rap. He spit spontaneous verses about traveling, his home back in California, and things we saw on the street.

We continued down to the town square again, this time viewing one of Prague's greatest tourist attractions, an ancient astronomical clock from the fifteenth century, located on the outside wall of the Old Town Hall on the corner of the square. Every hour, two trap doors would slide open and the twelve apostles, in the form of large figurines about a foot tall, would parade past the open doors to the wonderment of onlookers below. The clock itself was decorated with ornate skeletons dancing on vines. It made for a trippy, fantasy packed display of Christianity.

After clock gazing, we transitioned into a game of hacky sack. Many hours were passed along the course of the trip juggling the knit sack full of beads back and forth. Often times other pedestrians became interested in our game. We would form a circle and welcome them to join in. It was an easy way to meet people and one of many ways for us to occupy our free time.

Time is the greatest commodity a person has when they are traveling carelessly across the European continent. Normally accustomed to the fast pace lifestyle of America, this was a period when we had all the time we could possibly want to partake in whatever we wanted. We remained unbounded by responsibility or limitation of schedule. Every street, every train station, and every park was an opportunity. Our actions were dictated only by our own whimsy.

This newfound freedom was difficult to reconcile at first. Evan and I were still adjusting from the schedule we had been adhering to all summer. On the book field, every day begins at 5:59am with a cold shower. We got up a minute before 6am as sign of mental toughness, theoretically one upping the competition. The cold shower helps you wake up at such an ungodly hour. After packing a quick lunch you head to the breakfast head-quarters, usually a small mom and pop shop diner, for a hearty meal with your roommates. Before you know it, you are at the first door knocking before 8am. The rest of the day consists of setting up brief twenty-minute presentations with customers. The goal is to demonstrate the books to thirty families per day. It takes a lot of discipline and focus to get these demonstrations completed by 9:30pm when we close shop. This schedule continued from Monday to Saturday. On Sunday we stayed busy running training meetings and holding personal conferences with our student sales-people. After three months of this hectic, never ending labor, it takes some time to assimilate back to a normal schedule. The transition from the summer to backpacking was, to say the least, drastic.

I was delighted in watching the strangers' faces, especially the children, lighting up with joy when the clock tower came to life. Euphorically, we kicked the small woven bag around without a worry in our minds. At one point, Evan and I encouraged an old couple of non-English speaking tourists to let us take a picture of them "raising the roof", pumping their open hands up and down in the air above their heads like the professional basketball players in the NBA were doing at the time. They wore smiles from ear to ear and youthful enthusiasm on their faces. Directly following that shot we had them take one of us giving the same ridiculous pose. It remains one of my favorites.

After many heroic saves and valiant diving efforts, we heard the sharp, piercing notes of a Dixieland band strumming in the nearby distance. We moseyed over to see what it was all about, becoming entranced by a quartet of old timers playing ragtime. The band was midway through "Hello Dolly," a classic tune covered by Louis Armstrong in the musical of the same name. They twanged on with a few more tracks, speaking briefly in between songs. What struck us was how much pleasure they took in entertaining the crowd. There weren't many people paying attention, but the men jammed on obliviously with gleeful visages, fully engaged in their instruments. Each guy took his turn at a solo. The drummer played a rudimentary set of water bottles, along with an acoustic bass, a flute, and a singer with a megaphone. He was scattin' and slurrin' his words with a youthful mojo. An Irish bloke named Kevin, whom we met while hacking, said it best:

"How great it would be to take such pleasure in life at such an old age."

He was absolutely right, these men were at least in their seventies, but you could not put an age on the type of fun they were having. The six of us, Evan, Andy, Lucas, Kevin, his girlfriend Dona, and I danced our own sort of jig as the serendipitous sun broke through the clouds and shone down on our happy heads.

Soon the positive vibes from our little party attracted two other young backpackers from Austria named Indie and Christian. Indie, the more outspoken of the two, wore medium length dread locks wrapped up in a brown cloth tied around his head. Christian sported a shaved head with a strange pink tail hanging from the back. They told us they were driving around Europe in a Winnebago they had purchased from one of their parents, and invited us to join them in the "van down by the river." All except Andy, who was getting a fancy Thai massage, followed the Austrians to their vehicle parked under a highway overpass. We partook in a few joints and cold beers. The delicious 24 oz. beers, called Krusevic, cost only twenty krowns, or about two dollars. Somehow we started calling the currency "kroner" that day and the name stuck. That's how we referred to our money for the rest of the trip regardless of the country.

We all communed for the next few hours down at the van drinking, smoking, telling stories and generally just clowning around. The

Austrians regaled us with tales of life on the road, specifically Indie, the more gregarious of the two, who also demonstrated his formidable talents in freestyle rhyming. He could rap both in English and German. His German verses sounded mysterious and calculated.

There was something liberating about meeting and befriending these random people. It was the sense of acceptance and camaraderie inherent in the traveler's spirit. It enables you to meet people freely and behave in a fully uninhibited fashion. In everyday life, people tend to build walls around themselves. More concerned about being judged and fitting in, they metamorphosis into what they feel they ought to be, or what they think others want them to be. Here we were open and expressive, acting as our unencumbered true selves. That was what was so magical about our crew, everybody fit in, everybody mattered, and everybody could be him or herself. Even Christian, who proved to be a little bit less open-minded, and was actually more weird and scary than anything. His outlook was dour, almost nihilist, so I guess you could say that he didn't totally fit in, but we all acted like he did anyway.

We became hungry when the sun went down and so meandered back to town to mow down on some noodles at a ridiculously well lit Taiwanese dinner. The Austrians just sat and watched us eat. I assume it was because they were on a tighter budget. Afterwards we found a pub with a row of long wooden tables outside where we could all sit together. We ordered up some more beers and drank to our heart's content. Everything was going well until a group of about ten German guys sat down next to us. Indie was scribbling verses relentlessly in Evan's journal, but he stopped when they arrived. They were swilling beers and chanting drinking songs. Apparently the blatant show of machismo was not to his liking, because he began to berate them openly, mockingly chanting, "We are zee stupid Germans, Neanderthal buffoons, rah, rah, rah!"

The rest of us were dumbfounded and slightly uncomfortable. They could have easily bounced our crew, but somehow Indie knew they wouldn't. We carried on laughing and drinking without incident. I was pretty much out of gas from the long day so I walked back with Andy to our hostel. Before retiring, I ducked into the Internet café to write an email to my girl Heidi back in Milwaukee. It was actually a poem, which flowed fluidly and naturally from my fingertips. The gist of it was how excited I was by our new liaison and how I could not stop thinking about her even though she was half a world away. It was well received and she wrote back quickly confirming that she too was ready for love. I went to bed that night feeling well.

The next day Andy caught a train for a jaunt up into Poland and another region of the Czech Republic called Cesky Krumlov. We saw him off at the station, agreeing to reunite for Oktoberfest in a week. Evan and I shipped off en route to the city of music, Vienna, Austria. The day of travel was a good time for us to reconvene, reevaluate, and relive the events of the trip to date. He was pretty much in the same state of mind as I was. Fully engaged and enlivened.

When we arrived in Vienna the weather took a turn for the worse. Having not booked a hostel ahead of time, we had to hike around town in the rain trying to find accommodation. Carrying protective covers for our bags was not a precaution that had occurred to us. We traipsed through the city, wet and dejected, not really knowing where to look. In every other location we were able to find a hostel quickly and easily, if not from our travel book then simply from inquiring from the locals. But with everyone indoors because of the precipitation, we had a hard time finding assistance. After a couple of hours and some backtracking, we finally found the Koplinghaus Miedling, a dormitory style

79

building that suited our needs. We played a quick game of Gin Rummy before retiring at about 8pm, not waking until eleven hours later. Clearly we needed to catch up on our Zzzs. In the morning we felt refreshed and alert. We celebrated our gusto by destroying the complimentary breakfast of granola cereal, toast, jam, orange juice, and coffee.

To get downtown we caught the underground metro, which dropped us at the Ring Boulevard. Commissioned by emperor Franz Josef in 1857, the Ring encompasses the entire city center in a big circle. The first thing we noticed in Vienna was how immaculate the train system was. Everything was perfectly spotless and clean, the people prim and proper. In fact the entire city was well groomed and tidy. We took a nice stroll along the Boulevard and through the museum district to behold the awesome structural beauty.

The tranquil day took a turn for the bizarre when we stopped at an Internet café. First off, the rate for use was $6 per hour (the most I had paid prior was $2). Secondly, I discovered that Heidi had written a strange, rambling diatribe of an email the night before after a trip on mushrooms with some mutual friends back in Milwaukee. The message was difficult to decipher and I left confused. My confusion continued when Evan and I walked past a storefront window. Inside were about twenty manikins. There was a frantic little, old man dressed like the mad hatter running around adjusting their clothes. What the hell was he in such a hurry for? Was I stuck in the movie *Alice in Wonderland*?

The final incident this afternoon was discovering a statue of a horse with the American flag painted on it that had been violently knocked to the ground. Across the city, various artists had decorated these horse statues as some type of commemorative art gesture, the same way large cow statues popped up with a plethora of patterns and designs in the city of Chicago in the late nineties. We had seen plenty of others on our walk that morning, but this particular horse lay vandalized next to the podium where it once stood, only its hooves in tact. Apparently someone pissed off at the United States had walked by, perhaps in a drunken state, and decided we did not deserve a horse statue. Being that this was only two years after the 9/11 attacks on the World Trade Center, there were strong emotions all over the world about America. These emotions were made worse when our government decided to start a misguided war with "terrorists" in Afghanistan. Somehow we ended up in Iraq as well and things got very messy.

Although this act of vandalism was not a big deal per se, it still hurt our feelings. We were young and idealistic but not foolish enough to think that our country was more sacred than any other or our people any better. However, I believe that we still retained a sense of patriotic pride instilled in us by our society. This part of us was wounded by what we saw. We were stunned because it was not a place you would expect to see such a rude gesture. Everything and everyone here appeared so polished, respectful, and polite.

Discombobulated from the day's events, we decided it would be wise at this unusual time to find our way to our favorite refuge and toss the Frisbee. We could always count on a beautiful aesthetic at the park, and it was no different at the Volksgarten. A flat open plane adorned with a rose garden, temple and monument, the Volksgarten, or people's garden, was built over the fortifications that Napoleon destroyed during his conquest of Europe. Now it assumes an idyllic, peaceful quality. On this day the grass was radiating bright green in the sun. The vibe here was much more relaxed than Amsterdam or Prague; the cleanliness and calm a welcome contrast. We had been enjoying the bustle and nightlife of other cities, but the slower pace of Vienna was a welcome respite.

Running around barefoot chasing the Frisbee on the well-groomed lawn helped clear our heads. Afterwards we sat watching dogs frolic and play. We met a scampy young mutt that we obviously called Eddy, who was bouncing around with Allie, a happy little sparkplug of a Jack Russell terrier. They found a yellow Lab to jam with, and then a ferocious Dachshund joined in the mix. Last in was a Paraguayan pup named Nanu, with an owner called Andreas. Watching dogs play together in a park, while such a seemingly simple activity, is actually quite fascinating. Essentially, they size each other up the same way that we humans do. First they sneak up for a quick sniff, for us a hand-shake and friendly introduction, then they feel each other out by running around getting familiar, the equivalent of conversation. The only real difference is that dogs do not have any logical sense of reason in which to judge one of their own. Their reaction is based on instinct rather than any kind of mindful deduction. The dogs would rotate from playing with each other, to sidling over towards us to say hello, and then back to their canine counterparts. It was a peaceful communing of beast and man. We had a nice time just kick-ing back, watching nature carry on with and around us.

Later, a couple of local guys asked us if they could play some Frisbee. Apparently it's not such a common thing to do in Vienna. Jackel, pronounced Yackel, a twenty-year-old native, and his friend, who was much quieter, began inquiring about our trip. He was a very intelligent marketing manager for EMI/Virgin, a massive record label in Britain. He had just received a promotion, but was feeling burned out by the whole industry. Jackel was a wise man, profound in his advice and informative about his city. Out of the kindness of his heart, or inspired by a great sense of pride and duty as a devoted Austrian, he and his friend gave us a marvelous walking tour of the city center. They pointed out the historical significance of certain buildings, such as one that was occupied by Adolph Hitler and his cronies before taking over the Nazi party in Germany.

The tour was capped off by a stop at a chic corner café later in the evening to grab a couple of beers and continue our discussions on various topics. He advised us that true happiness, in his eyes, comes from following the path that your heart tells you to follow, pursuing the dreams that you have deep down inside. When you stay true to these emotional purposes, he said, you will experience greater contentment than you would trying to make your friends or family happy. These words struck a chord within us, because these were the types of answers we were seeking on this trip.

It was a Sunday night. They both had to work early, yet continued to host us and make sure that we got an acute sense of life and culture in Vienna. There was no motive for them to entertain us. I think their interest in our trip was more a case of wishing they had the freedom to pack a bag and go explore the world as well. Or possibly they were just lonely, as most of their friends had already established relationships and families. They probably had no one to go home to. Ultimately, I believe they were enforcing the golden rule, treating us the way they would want to have been treated if they were in a foreign land.

Most young Europeans can relate well to backpackers because they have grown up close to the endless litany of high quality travel destinations across their continent. Many have had the opportunity to travel internationally on family vacations, high school graduation trips, or holidays with friends. Growing up in the states, travel and lodging are so much more expensive. Safe budget accommodation is hard to find. Everything is spread out, so distance also becomes a challenge.

Also, Americans have a comparatively similar sense of history and culture throughout the nation. There are some obvious distinctions, i.e., the North vs. South, or East Coast vs. West Coast, but everyone generally watches the same television programs and movies, reads the same books, and speaks English. In Europe, your neighbor next door may speak a different language, or a dialect of the same language, possess an entirely different set of cultural norms, and more often than not, has been a mortal enemy of your people for hundreds of years. These distinctions make Europe an unparalleled location for travel. Nowhere in the world does such variation of climates, cultures, and histories exist in such a constricted, navigable area.

On Monday morning, Evan was not feeling very well. We found another park, Burggarten, to relax for the day before jumping on an afternoon train to the home of the Magyar people, Budapest, Hungary. Inspired by my leisure, I wrote the following poem:

Take a journey in this place,
Through questions, patient thoughts,
On hills and plains congruent

Where time has no constraint,
To ponder or lounge,
Relax; stretch your weary back

Take burden off the soul,
Watch canine float and play,
In an instinctive way

Jumbled strings of your conscious untangle,
You become entangled,
You may reap what's expected,
Or become perplexed in this session

If an ultra violet ray obliges,
The trip that you take,
Will be blessed with its paint

The canopy may hold clear,
And you hope this pleasant ceiling,
Won't shed tears unyielding

Just as Freud, and thinkers alike,
Must've treasured these paths,
Walked freely in delight

Artists and paupers join,
Reunited by human likeness,
Comforted, or lost right then,
Controlled by new forces

Wicked winds may blow here,
But not on a day,
Compiled with such niceties,
Never to destroy sublime

The journey out of Austria began by taking the metro to the wrong side of town. We
laughed at ourselves for our naiveté but soon
met a friendly Norwegian guy who helped us
locate the correct station, as well as pique
our excitement about Budapest. He had just
spent a week there and had a great stay. Now
he had to return to Bergen, Switzerland to
continue his studies. Of all the locations on

our itinerary, this was certainly the one we knew least about. The only reason we included it was out of its sheer proximity to Austria.

"Why not add another country to the list?"

Turning around to ride back through town, we boarded a nice, clean train car and had a short, comfortable ride of two hours into Hungary. Getting sicker by the moment, Evan slept the whole way there. Upon exiting at the platform we were physically grabbed by an old lady who propositioned us with a place to stay, not with her, but with an even older lady named Irene. We were weary about the credibility of someone who seemed so desperate to house backpackers, insisting that it would be much nicer in Irene's "apartment" than at a hostel. Also we were cautious about the old bait and switch tactic. It turned out that she was just a translator. Irene's English was spotty at best. Her friend was only being helpful. "What are the chances of being swindled by a nice old lady," we thought, and decided to roll the dice. The price was right, as well, only twenty-five Euros per night for the both of us in a private room.

The second floor apartment had three rooms and a shared bathroom. We were the only ones currently staying. It was quite nice, fitted with high ceilings, wood flooring, and two separate single beds made up with plenty of blankets and pillows. It was exactly the type of bedding you would expect an old lady to have; rosy, flowered patterns with bright pink and purple wool blankets. We didn't mind the femininity of the place, but if we met any girls that wanted to come back with us they would probably think we lived with our grandma. Dusk slowly settled into the Hungarian sky. By this time Evan was feeling downright miserable. Irene finished showing us all the pertinent details of the apartment and explaining everything, not with words but pointing gestures. Evan settled in to get some rest. I went out on my own to explore the town.

It was fully dark when I hit the street. The city had fallen into a languid, passive daze. Most of the stores in the area had already closed for the day. It was eerie in fact. There were very few people moving about on the sidewalk and no lights on any of the buildings. All the businesses had shut their windows. I began to wonder if we were in an unsafe area. Looking around I decided it was more calm and quiet than it was dangerous. The silence actually created an ambience that was tranquil. You can never be too careful in a new environment. Perhaps the reason I felt comfortable was that on every second street corner or alleyway I passed on my casual walk, young couples were kissing, hugging, and grop- ing each other as if there were an imminent citywide relationship strike looming. I had never seen so many people freely express-ing their emotions in public before. I dubbed Budapest the PDA (public display of affection) capital of Europe. On the train, in the street, left and right a make out free-for-all.

Unfortunately, the overt display of love made me miss Heidi. We had talked nearly every day of that summer and now it had been about two weeks since I had heard her sweet voice. I would find a calling card and phone her in the morning for sure. I noticed that the women in Budapest were pound for pound a heavier lot than those in Prague.

"It must be the Goulash," I thought.

Back at the apartment, once voyeurism got old, Evan was lying in a pool of his own sweat, groaning and looking altogether unwell. I hoped he would improve by morning and was fortunately not disappointed. He had acquired some kind of twenty-four-hour virus and just needed to perspire it out of his body. Come sunup he was good to go. My sidekick has a most resilient nature, let me tell you. You can knock a Quackenbush down, but you cannot knock him out; believe that.

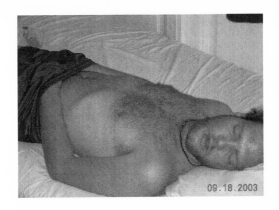

09.18.2003

In the morning we were greeted by clean,
fresh air and a cloudless sky that we had not
seen since our first day in Amsterdam. Our old
friend the sun was dancing like a happy orange
on the horizon. Nonchalantly we walked down-
stairs to the lower level of the large, yellow
train station just up the street from our new
domicile and found a breakfast stand that was
selling croissants and pastries for mere pennies. We washed these treats down with tiny
shots of Espresso in little white plastic dis-
posable Solo cups. I think we paid something
like seventy cents for three pastries and two
coffees. After eating we had a seat outside
on the round cement stools situated in the
middle of the open-air square with small shops
selling cheap handbags and other trinkets. We
kicked back to take in the morning bustle of
commuter traffic.

A few seats over the International Confederation of Eastern Bloc Gypsies were convening for their daily meeting. There were nine or ten of them present, mostly middle aged, with very dark, wrinkly red faces and black beady eyes glazed over by the first couple swigs of vodka or gin. Their heads were mostly wrapped in thin, worn handkerchiefs, their bodies in dingy pants and weathered skirts. They carried beat up old rucksacks containing whatever few personal belongs were necessary. The ragtag bunch had little for possessions but they seemed to be enjoying themselves immensely. Lively and playfully they poked and prodded each other, laughing, smiling ebullient gap toothed smiles at the warm sun. A couple of them were occupied with a game of chess. The others cackled back and forth in an unintelligible foreign tongue. I am not sure we would have understood much of what was being said even if we had spoken fluent Hungarian. It reminded us of the "mumble grumble" guy back in Amsterdam, but much less serious. Ironically, we felt like we actually fit in better with these folks than those professionals who were wearing suits and going to work. I was perfectly content with that.

The city of Budapest is divided down the middle by the Danube River; the north side being called Buda, and the south side simply Pest. Buda has a more industrialized, working-class vibe; the South is a higher scale region, both geographically and economically. Here you find a greater population of restaurants, art museums, and wealthier, upscale neighborhoods. To cross the river you walk across a grand bridge, past a well-landscaped roundabout that controls the flow of traffic from the main street running perpendicular. Upon crossing, and looking back across the river eastward is the massive, grandiose burgundy roofed complex of the Hungarian National Parliament. It's a gothic beige colored facade resting on the banks of the Danube on the Buda side. The marvelous, cast iron Szechenyi Chain Bridge, which glows with lights in the evening, sits adjacent. Straight down the bank, on the Pest side, the darker, grayish Buda Castle and Matthias Church overlook the river. In the background is a range of dark hills that rise into the distance. In between the hill and the Castle is a small forest of trees and other foliage buffering the water. The best view of the city is available from the summit of a formidable ledge at a park called Gellert Hill. This was surely the gem of our stay in town.

A steady, zigzagged climb to the top took about a half hour. Turning around to look down we were startled by the beauty of the whole scene. From above, the river appeared tranquil and unassuming, yet stoic and knowledgeable.

Its dark brown tint sent earthy shades upwards toward the bridges and buildings lining its shore, pronouncing a serious, harrowing tone. Also occupied by the Soviets during the Cold War, the city speaks to many years of oppression and sadness, but also of new horizons and hope. Not as popular for tourism, and not as architecturally diverse as Prague, Budapest is more like the less attractive cousin who prides itself on its experience, its wisdom, and knack for survival. We were already happier there than in the Czech Republic simply because of the amount of sunshine. Having no prior expectations left us in the perfect position to be pleasantly surprised.

At the summit of Gellert Hill we ran into a large tour group. They were dropping coins in the telescopic machines that offered a magnified view of the city. Generally disinterested in mingling with large groups, we chose to get away from the crowd as soon as possible. But not before discovering our new most favorite snack, the Solero power ice treat. It's no more than a simple, frozen stick of flavored juice, but with sweat forming on our brow and a damp stickiness to our t-shirts, the power treat was a superb delicacy. We ended up consuming about ten more each in the next three days. Thank God for the good folks at Solero.

After tossing the Frisbee for a good hour, running it down amongst resplendent beds of tulips, we each meandered separate ways to find a good spot to journal. The well-manicured gardens that speckled the park with vibrancy and glee blended well with the wide-open fields of grass. It felt as if the park had been designed just for us.

Following the trails to the backside of the hill I found the rock of my dreams. This rock was magical. Perhaps not as mystically powerful as the happy nut I clutched so tightly during my mushroom trip; it was something else in size. It was big enough that I could lie down in the supine position without my legs or head dangling over the side, and flat enough to still be comfortable. Happily warmed by the midday sun, I took off my shirt and lay out to take in some cozy rays and empty my brimming head of a multitude of thoughts and ideas. The two hours I spent reclined on that rock, we'll call it "Gary," were some of the happiest moments of my trip. I wrote a couple of poems about my dear lady friend of whom I could not stop thinking about, all the while listening to my favorite musical companions on the Discman.

I am referring to The Grateful Dead. I was not a huge fan of The Dead before Europe, probably because I had not been very well exposed to their music. There was something blissful and soothing about the tunes coming out of my headphones from that live three-disc show in

New Jersey in 1977. I would say that my love for their music and Jerry Garcia, lead singer/guitarist, began here. Sheer jubilation and joy sprang from his guitar, nothing but soul in his scratchy, warm, kind, honest, desperate, angelic voice. He sang with sadness and depth, about the trials and tribulations not only of the band itself, but seemingly every person in the world. The songs were empathetic, telling stories of hope in the face of hardship, happiness in the times of sorrow. The lessons felt directly applicable to my life at the time. I was linked to the emotions in the music in my own personal journey.

Most importantly, his songs were sung with heart. A majority were love songs, if not about a specific woman, then a love for life. They would play a pertinent role in my travels, enabling my mind to wander into chasms of serendipity as well as hollows of despair. The entire emotional spectrum was captured in that three-disc set. Mostly it was positive, and I reached levels of elation and contentment that were musically foreign to me. Whenever I hit a rough patch I knew I just had to keep on "Truckin."

After the music ran out on the disc in my player I continued to sit in stillness. A meditative trance overcame me and I became very aware of my breathing, fully sensing the amazement that is the human body. My skin felt alive in the sun, almost as if it were breathing its own air independently. I began to sense my body in its form, my thoughts and feelings a completely separate entity. I was a corporal being undergoing an ethereal existence. There was a flow of energy throughout my body that felt as if it was coming from some greater force than me. Oxygen pulsed throughout my blood stream. I could feel and see it in my mind. It was a fully spiritual sensation in which time was suspended, consciousness elevated. Each system in my body seemed aligned, working together as one. This sense of peace and lightness, of extreme well-being lasted just a few moments but when I opened my eyes I felt cleansed, refreshed, and new. I could not help but grinning as I said goodbye to Gary and thanked him for what he had shown me.

In the late afternoon we reconvened. By the smile on the face of the happy Norwegian, I could tell he had had an equally pleasant time exploring the depths of his consciousness. All that thinking caused us great hunger, so we slid back down the hill, to the lower lands of Pest, and found the restaurant district. On a side street right next to the river we grubbed down on a hearty plate of Goulash. After the combination of food and a flagon of wine, plus all the vitamin D soaked up at the park, we became groggy. We traveled bipedal back to the crib to get involved in some nap action. We both awoke after the sun had fallen from the sky and darkness had begun its turn with the clock. We jumped in the shower, separately of course, to clean up and revive ourselves before hitting the town. Oktoberfest was just around the corner and we were not nearly in the kind of drinking shape we would need to be in for the massive amounts of beer that were sure to be swilled. Feeling abnormally cultured, we bought a bottle of wine at the closest liquor store and eased into the night.

Later on, strolling along the banks of the river, I noticed a commotion on one of the large boats docked side to. Upon closer examination we saw that it was actually a club. For a small fee we were able to walk up the gangway and join a small group of young people dancing to house music on the upper level. It was only a Tuesday night, so the crowd never grew very big. We decided to come back on the weekend when it was packed full. On the walk home we found a quaint little casino. Being highly addicted to blackjack at the time, I sat down for one of many marathon sessions. The accepted currency was the local Furint, which had the feel of monopoly money because of its colorful, artsy design. The table minimum was the equivalent of about two and a half dollars, not too dangerous, and after a few nine-dollar Jack Daniels and cokes, I really started to roll. Evan is a much more logical gambler than I. After going up twenty bucks in a half hour, he folded up shop and took off to wander the streets.

I stayed until four in morning, when the manager finally said it was time to go. Evan had been unsuccessful at trying to coax me out earlier, explaining, "Wes, you're just going to lose all your money, don't do it, its too early in the trip."

Being the belligerent drunken gambler that I am, I paid no attention to his sound advice. Hours later the dealer was pleading with me to wrap it up, but I was relentless. Persistently I begged for one more shoe, and then one more shoe, until he finally had to put his foot down. I returned the next two nights to feed the monkey. The same dealer was working. We got to be pretty comfortable with one another. I was exaggerating my obnoxious American tourist routine intentionally, which he seemed to like. Luckily, he never protested when I started smoking hash joints with tobacco towards the end of the night. Probably because he was enjoying watching me throw my money away. Each night he had to kick me out after all the other casino patrons had left. I was having too much fun to leave on my own account. "It's four in the morning sir, can I please go home," he protested.

"Ok, ok, I'm sorry," I apologized.

I decided I had had enough. It was time to cut myself off.

Besides revisiting Gellert Hill and destroying copious amounts of Salero Power Treats, most of our daytime activity involved lounging at the public bathhouses. There were five main baths in town. For us it was the perfect way to pass the days in a city without as much museum or tourist fodder. The first one we visited was the largest in town. It was a big, yellow stucco recreation facility that charged only five dollars for the day. There were locker rooms inside for changing and showering, as well as receiving massages. What followed was a series of rooms with all different sizes and shapes of pools of varying temperatures and mineral concentrations. The minerals function as exfoliating agents that cure and soften the skin.

The ceilings were high, arching domes, and the building itself was over two hundred years old. Some pools had a brownish tint on account of the solvents, others whooshed around in circles and carried your body effortlessly around. After jumping into every pool in the place, from hot to cold to tepid and back, we relaxed outside at the double-sided Olympic-sized pool. The locals were all sunbathing and lounging. They even had chess boards built into pedestals at the edge of the pool where old gray men with sagging bellies sat pondering their rookery and pawn foolery. Walking out after a three-hour mega soak we felt like a million Kroner, well refreshed, purged of all the toxins from the night before, and ready to put some more gruel into our gullets before hitting up the town again in the velvety twilight hours.

On the outskirts of Gellert Hill sat a large old hotel building across the street from the park. An ornately decorated gold arch doorway on the front façade supported the large gold dome roof. More expensive and exclusive, the Gellert Hill baths were even more astounding due to the sophisticated design of the pools. There were fancy stone ledges, Doric columns, and stain glass windows in the main foyer. The ambience resonated in obscurity with slender light forms poking in from outside. In the faintest of daylight we saw a few women bathing topless in the coed pools. This was highly exciting. You never get to see breasts in public in the States.

There were, however, separate complexes for men and women. On our side the only thing you wore over your critical parts was a small, white square canvas cloth of no more than a foot by a foot in dimension. It was to be tied with strings around your waist, blocking your bits from the public eye, but not your crack.

I guess if I had to choose which part of the male anatomy I would prefer to have sheltered from my eyes, it would be the privates, but it was still discomforting trying to hide from the omnipresent, blazing stare of so many vertical smiles. We considered paying for a massage, deciding it would be uncomfortable having a man rub our bodies with hot oil after this much male ass exposure. Instead we contented ourselves with just soaking in the absurdity of a room full of men wearing nothing but hanker chiefs.

We had only planned on staying for three days in Budapest, but were having so much fun lounging at the bathhouses and soaking in the positive vibrations on the Gellert Hill, that we extended our stay for two more days. The extra time also allowed for a reunion of the finest order with our Okie friend Andy. His time in the Czech Republic and Poland had treated him well. He informed us that the Polish girls were by far the most beautiful of any country in the world. "Seriously dudes, you've gotta go… I'm not kidding."

He claimed to have made out with a girl in Warsaw who was out of this world. It was tempting to reroute our two-month itinerary to witness "the hottest girls ever," but we didn't. We lead him across the river to a chill little café that we had discovered the prior day on the Buda side. The topic of girls continued and we got into a deep nostalgic conversation. Andy suggested we write out a list of all of our sexual experiences for memories' sake. It was hilarious remembering some of the ridiculous drunken hookups we had had throughout our high school and college years, as well as more innocent ones back in junior high. For Evan and me many of the names were the same. We raised our glasses and drank "To all the girls we had loved before."

As per usual, this night found me again at the casino irritating the staff and tossing my kroner to the wind. Andy and Evan wandered around looking for trouble in town. Unfortunately, I missed the interaction they had with some of the gypsies that were hanging around outside of one of the liquor stores. After trying to communicate unsuccessfully in drunken English, they began speaking gibberish back and forth in an attempt to further confuse the tramps. Yelling at each other fervently and aggressively in a completely nonsensical, fabricated tongue. Not to be outdone, the gypsies eventually faded into the night. I was sorry to have missed it but did enjoy the speaking their gypsy language throughout the next day.

Feeling fully maxed out on the great country of Hungary, my comrade and I shipped out, saying goodbye to Andy again, parting company for only two days this time until reconvening in Munich. For the first and only time we made reservations before arriving. Word on the street was that Oktoberfest was an intense, highly crowded affair and we would be unable to find a bed in any of the hostels. We forked over an excessive forty dollars a night to sleep in a tent on a campground a couple of miles from the city. This required us to walk about twenty minutes to get the metro into town and shower under cold streams of drizzle. As long as we had a place to pass out with a belly full of beer at the end of the night we would be happy.

To kill a couple of days before Munich, we stopped in the idyllic city of Zurich, Switzerland, smack dab in the middle of Western Europe. It's conveniently located for a short stay before the big festival. Known for its historic neutrality from international war and conflict, home to the United Nations and most of the largest private banks in the world, a foreign tax haven, and winter wonderland for skiers; Switzerland is an incomparable experience. It was easy to explain why the Swiss are so harmonious once we spent a few hours in Zurich.

It felt as if all the stress and anxiety that floats through the air in our advanced, modern world, unnamed and unstated, was sucked out through a giant vacuum hose in the sky as we departed from the train and stepped out into the city center. As if a burden we were unaware of had been lifted off our tired shoulders. Whispering yellow rays of cracked sunshine bounced off the chlorophyll clogged vines climbing the ancient wall of the clock tower at the center of the town. On the street, people were peaceful, wearing contented, natural grins on their faces. They walked patiently and unhurried. No one seemed to be pressed for time, uneasy, or even remotely troubled. The Swiss bring serenity in civilization to a higher level. The exquisite brown cobblestone street we perused for a place to sleep was totally devoid of even the slightest speck of litter. Locals sat pleasantly enjoying their meals at the cafes and restaurants. The buildings were all craftily, quaintly designed, as if constructed from a fairytale blueprint. This was to be the ideal place to spend two days relaxing before the big festival. That evening we purchased some groceries and cooked our own pasta at the hostel. Despite the plentiful variety of fine dining establishments on the promenade, there was not much in the way of budget fare. Dining on the cheap and counting our blessings, we could not believe how handsomely fortune was treating us.

In the morning I made my most significant purchase of the trip at a tidy little stationary store on the river. It was a hardcover journal with VanGogh's *Terasse des Cafes an der Place du Forum in Arles am Abend*. It's the one with a bright orange and yellow café at night on a cobblestone alley with powerful, dark shades forming the surrounding buildings and night-time sky. This book would serve me better as a daily log than the flip top pad of paper that I had bought at the Van Gogh museum in Amsterdam. It would last for a couple of years after the trip, chronicling my entire relationship with Heidi and subsequent trav-els through South America. Now armed with the proper accoutrements of a contemplative backpacker, I began anew, ready to capture my ensuing passions, hopes, thoughts, and dreams.

Writing is something I have always enjoyed. I remember being encouraged in English by my teachers in school. One of the proudest accomplishments in my life was receiving a second place ribbon in the 6th grade young authors competition for my story, *Jake's Sad Life*. It was an epic saga about a young boy who had to endure a painful childhood full of foster parents and orphanages, heartache and broken dreams. Finally catching a break by being adopted by a happy, loving family, he tragically crashes his brand new go-cart into a tree. Lying in the hospital, a heap of bro-ken bones, Jake contemplates the reality of a harsh world. I guess I understood at a young age that drama sells.

This trip was the first time I had kept a proper journal. In the beginning I would simply jot down a few bullet points about the highlights of any given day, where we went, what we saw, what cool people we met. Evan, I noticed, was telling a more thorough story in his journal, a cork covered booklet purchased prior to the trip. Over time I developed a style more in his vein. When constructing this memoir many years after the fact, his perceptions and recollections were paramount to telling the whole story. Reading both journals allowed me to see things more vividly. Many times he had excerpts from experiences I had completely forgotten, listed names that had slipped my mind with time, or simply offered a unique assessment of the same experience, shedding extra light on what my own perceptions had been. I am grateful for having maintained this habit throughout subsequent travels. It has allowed me to chronicle my past in striking detail. Looking back through these narrations, poems, quotations, to-do lists, goals, and songs, has enriched my life tremendously. I look forward to hopefully sharing them with my children one day, the family friendly entries at least. An old woman on an airplane one time told me that writing is a sign of intelligence. That is why I sometimes pull out my journal just to try and look smart.

A beautiful, sunny morning with clear, blue skies and fluffy white clouds inspired us to get some exercise. We could not believe our ears when the gentleman at the tourism office in the train station informed us that we could rent a cruiser bicycle for the day for FREE. "You mean nothing at all," Evan asked dumbfounded.

"Yes, yes," he said, "all we need is your passports and you are free to go."

Killer. We grabbed a fresh set of wheels and rode off along a gravel path forged about the giant lake at the head of town, Lake Zurich. It was also the name of a town and high school back in the Chicago suburbs in our sports conference back in Crystal Lake. Evan was a local basketball hero who held the record for the most three-pointers in school history. Granted these happened to be the first two years of the high school's history, and the record was quickly broken. I was a golfer and held the record for most clubs thrown in match play. I was awarded a three-match suspension for my efforts. By now our names have surely faded into high school history.

We spent the middle of the day lazily riding, stopping intermittently to walk into the frigid water, which came just up to our knees.

Just enough to feel the gripping autumn chill of the transparent, blue waters. We stopped off at a cantina in the middle of an expansive city park to enjoy delicious cafeteria-style bratwursts with French fries for lunch. Correction: Freedom fries. While munching our yummy hot sausages we noticed a group of young people, probably a few years our seniors, lounging on blankets, sunbathing, and smoking joints. After lunch we found a bench a few yards from the lakeside and blended into the scenery. Two of the women were topless, and the thinner, blond girl was absolutely stunning.

"How cool it is to sit unassumingly in public, watching gorgeous women frolicking seminude in the afternoon sun? I could probably get used to this place, how bout you?"

"Uhhhhhhhh, yeah," he replied effortlessly.

After lunch we hung around the park reading and watching the sunshine dance licentiously upon the unassuming water. Adjacent to our lookout on the lake was a perfectly flat pitch of luscious grass. I noticed there were three guys throwing a Frisbee. They all had their shirts off, exposing exceptionally tanned, muscular forms. They must have been standing close to two and fifty feet away from each other in a triangle and were whipping the disc through the sky with incredible force and accuracy. Each throw landed perfectly in the next ones hands. They floated parallel to the earth on an invisible rope across the sky. Forehands and backhands, all thrown with deadly aim. Their windup was extreme and skillful, like a coil. Their well-sculpted bodies reminded me of Ancient Greeks Olympians launching a discus. Rather than tainting the quality of play with our amateur talent we just sat in awe of their precision.

As in Amsterdam, smoking marijuana is very common in Switzerland. It's not technically legal, but society generally turns a blind eye to its consumption and sale. You get a certain sense that the rules are swept under the rug, allowing people to do what they want as long as they are not causing a problem. It's possible to purchase it in shops in town, but on a much more clandestine basis. We found ours at another head shop that sold Buddhist trinkets and incense. When we asked if they sold pot, the lady said, "No, but we sell tea," winking knowingly across the counter.

The product is a natural outdoor strain, not the generally more potent indoor, hydroponically grown cannabis. Its consistency is much drier and leafier, rather than fluffy, dense buds. Apparently by marketing it as a tea to be consumed in drink form, they keep the authorities satisfied. Somehow a loophole exists, but the proprietor of the store was "hush, hush" about selling it to us. She informed us that it is not technically legal to be carrying in the streets. This grass was far better for rolling in joints, easier to break apart, and not quite as strong. Rather than an intense, heady "stoned" affect, it gave us more of a light-headed body buzz, and a case of the giggles. It was a nice change of pace from the super strong nuggets we were still carrying with us from Holland. Between the hash, indoor, and outdoor weed, we had amassed quite a nice little stash. The fact that carrying cannabis across international borders is illegal was of no concern. We were on a journey for freedom, damn it, nobody was going to tell us what we could and could not do.

Settling into a four-hour train ride from our sensational two days of relaxation in Zurich (a vacation from our vacation, if you will) with the afternoon sunshine causing me to feel sleepy, I slipped off into dreamland. It would be an intense couple of days of partying coming up at Oktoberfest. Why is it called Oktoberfest when it takes place pre-dominately in September? I don't know. At any rate, my short rest abruptly came to an end when the passport agent tapped on my shoulder and asked for my identification. Scurrying half asleep through my daypack, which was sitting on the table between Evan and me, I found my trusty passport and handed it over casually. Expecting him to take it, peruse uneventfully, stamp and hand it back, I was instead met with a look of consternation as he picked up my small bag of "tea" between his thumb and forefinger.

"What is this?"

"Oh, that's tea," I tried saying as calmly and innocently as I could. His face remained serious. Looking over painfully to check Evan's reaction. I was greeted with an icy death stare.

"Come with me," he uttered succinctly. He then turned to Evan.

"Do you know him?" Although Evan was shaking his head back and forth in negation, it was clear that we were together.

We stood up, gathered our bags and walked up the length of the train car to the doorway. The disappointed agent lagged close behind. I had not had the feeling I experienced at that moment in a long time. It was the same one as when Evan and I were in sixth grade, walking down the hall, speaking ill of one of our classmates when our teacher walked out the door and heard me call her a "kiss ass." The same one that I felt when my dad found my "hash pipe" (no one called them hash pipes anymore) and cigarettes under the car seat in high school, and the same as when I was caught cheating at a high school golf tournament. It's the horribly uncomfortable realization that you have been caught. With the evidence dangling right there in front of your face, mocking you, snickering at your audacity. Only this time the stakes were much higher. I was not going to be handed an after school detention, grounded for a week, or suspended from the team for three matches. I had no idea what my punishment was going to be. Smuggling illegal drugs across international borders… "Oh Fuck."

After what seemed to be over an hour, but was probably only ten minutes, the train slowed gradually to a stop at the next station, Bregnol. When the doors opened two more agents were waiting for us on the platform. The three men lead us into the back quarters of their office, placed our backpacks onto a barren steel table, and began searching through every piece of clothing, toiletry case, and shopping bag looking for illicit substances. Of course it was not until the very end of the whole rigmarole that they unearthed the small plastic bags where we had lodged our goodies. As if this was not nerve-wracking enough, Evan was standing on the opposite side of the room berating me with every name in the book, essentially making sure I knew what a wretched piece of shit I was for being so careless with our dope. "Great hiding spot," he kept repeating sardonically.

I couldn't blame him really. I had put us at serious risk of being thrown in prison, deported, anally probed with Billy clubs, or whatever else was going to happen as a result of my folly. I was definitely feeling like a "dumb motherfucker." After every single one of our personal items had been laid out on the table and the officers were sure they had retrieved all of the evidence, they walked into the next room to weigh out all the separate quantities of hashish and cannabis, which they then noted on a sheet of paper at their desk. It was a thorough and comprehensive list.

Finally they came back into the room to ostensibly throw handcuffs on our miserable wrists and toss us in the clink. It was then that the almighty One smiled down on us. The man handed us our citations and told us in broken English we were free to leave. "Say what? That's it?"

Yes, that was it. They were merely interested in seizing our drugs and issuing citations. The man explained that the papers we held in our hands were tickets that would be sent home to our parents in the States.

"Oh, no. Please don't send a citation written in German to our English speaking parents," we laughed hysterically back at the station waiting for the next train to Munich.

Walking briskly out of the border patrol office our eyes met in an immediate gesture of unadulterated glee. It felt like we should high five, but I figured they were probably still watching and maybe it would be smart to play it cool. We weren't twenty feet away before our giggles became uncontrollable and we broke into full-blown guttural laughter. At the station we each bought a bottle of red wine and celebrated our regained freedom. I could not believe our luck. "I thought we were fucked, for sure," he chuckled mischievously.

"I'm sorry for all the things I said, but I just thought we were done."

I forgave him quickly and we took a picture of our souvenirs (tickets). Later on his brother Joel, who had taken German in high school, told us the papers said something about us being at risk of imprisonment if we were ever caught in Austria again with narcotics. No problem there, lesson learned. We got sufficiently buzzed off the wine and I rapidly began scribbling poetic lyrics about the incident into my notepad:

Riding the rails, two dogs without tails,
Forging trails, writing tales

Finding love, getting lost,
Trying to minimize the costs

Always high, often stoned,
Coffeeshops, stacking bones

Tabacco smoking, copious tokes and
Jokes, an unspoken oath

Young misfits getting pissed,
Drunken quips, bicycle tricks

Sack juggling, hash smuggling,
Funky adrenaline junkies

Glorious exploring, scoring,
Hearts pouring and soaring

Loving life, Imported Europeans,
In Museums, mental freedoms

The detour cost us a couple of hours so it
was nearly midnight by the time we located the
Thalkirchen campsite in Munich. After such an
eventful day it seemed wise to retire early so
as to save up as much energy as possible in
our stores for the three-day binge to come.
     Viva Los Rail Dogs!!!

Evan and I were amped for Oktoberfest for
a multitude reasons. Obviously we both love
drinking glasses of beer by the liter. Also,
Germany would be an exciting new country
with tradition and history to experience.
Most importantly, we would be meeting up with
our good friends Becky and Dee, who had also
sold books that summer with Southwestern.
They are the same age, had also just graduated University, both from The University
of Wisconsin-Lacrosse, and were traveling

Europe at the time. I would not say they were backpacking though. They had booked their trip through Contiki tours and were riding on a big tourist bus as part of a large organized group. We gave them a hard time for being lazy Americans. As they say, different strokes for different folks.

Becky was one of my best friends, having been a member of the same team my first summer. Her older sister Stacie had recruited us both and we had lived only a half an hour apart in Orlando, FL (aka Hades). It was so incredibly hot and humid that my polo shirt would be soaked with sweat by 9am. The ink on the pad of paper I carried around all day would smudge and wrinkle from the excessive perspiration emanating from the inside of my forearms. We left our cars back home in order to save money on gas, and therefore had to ride bicycles through our territories to get from door to door.

One specific day I was working with her roommate Laura, just to see an experienced dealer in action and to pick up some extra pointers. We dropped her off first thing in the morning before heading to work. I remember laughing my ass of when she rode off on her grandma bicycle with the huge nerd basket in front. The picture in my mind best resembled the scene in *The Wizard of Oz* when Miss Gulch is cruising over to Dorothy's house to steal Toto away for the malfeasance in her garden. The only difference was that instead of a mean scowl she wore a giant geek smile on her face, happier than a pig in shit to be riding her dorkmobile. That is what makes Becky great; she has never cared what people think about her. She does her own thing and knows who she is, albeit somewhat of a spaz, but she wears that badge with honor and always has a great attitude about life.

Evan knew Becky from that second summer in Pennsylvania when he and I lived together. Since she was a manager they got to know each other well in personal conferences on the selling field, as well as training meetings and incentive trips that were held throughout the school year. They had somewhat of a brother-sister relationship, whereas Becky and I had been a little bit more than friends. We were never officially a couple but spent a lot of time together over the years. We always got on really well, unless she got too drunk and I had to babysit her. Nobody plays the loud, obnoxious drunk card better.

The best times were on the "sizzler" trip that our company sponsored during the school year. Every salesperson who hit a certain level of sales over the summer was eligible to attend this vacation, which was held over the week of Thanksgiving. Hundreds of college students from all over the States would descend on exotic locations like Puerto Vallarta, Cancun, or Cabo San Lucas, Mexico for a week of debauchery. The trip was the ultimate experience of working with Southwestern company, who would foot half the bill for each student. Everyone would be talking about the craziness of sizzler for the rest of the year. It was always a huge motivation for working hard in the summer.

The girls happened to be staying at the same campgrounds so we met up with them early on our second day. That morning, when we were eating the hot breakfast provided to us by the tour company sponsoring the campsite, an Australian guy came up to Evan and asked in a heavy accent, "Oy, where'd you get the wicky mate?"

"I'm sorry?" He answered incredulously, having had no idea what "wicky" meant.

"Oy, the wicky! Where'd you get the wicky?"

"I don't know what you're talking about." The dude finally gave up and walked away. He was obviously inquiring about how we had scored food, a priceless commodity at the grounds, but Evan was not having his nonsense. We continued to mock the silly Aussie when he left. Later we realized he was asking about the "brekkie" or breakfast. This wasn't the first or last time I would struggle to understand what an Australian was saying.

The first day we headed in to the fair-grounds pretty early and ate a delicious lunch of Hendl (roast chicken) washed down with a liter of beer from heavy glass steins. These are the most common souvenirs from the festival. Many drunken patrons attempt to remove them stealthily from the tents. They are marked with each beer company's logo and are the standard serving size at the monstrous tents that litter the Theresienwiese. The festival has taken place annually since 1810, nearly two hundred years (not including two world wars), and was originally a celebration of marriage between Princess Therese Saxe-Hildburghausen and Prince Ludwig. It is the world's largest people's fair with over six million visitors over a sixteen-day span. Each brewery sponsors its own tent. The English speaking crowds generally hung out at the popular Hofbrauhaus, which we mostly avoided. The Lowenbrau tent had a statue of a twenty-foot tall lion whose mechanical arm rose to its mouth to take a drink every ten seconds. He was the thirstiest lion I have ever seen. Evan posed for a photo with a team of Clydesdale horses and a buggy lead by a middle-aged man in lederhosen.

Our favorite tent was the Augustiner. It's the local beer in Munich and has the most attractive tent. The hoppy ambrosia is served from individual wooden kegs rather than stainless steel vats. The women serving are spunky and energetic, donning dirndls; traditional dresses with skirts and aprons originally worn by Alpine peasants. Their bodices, worn under their blouses, fit extremely tight around the waist and push their breasts up nearly into their chins. It's not uncommon to see them carrying ten steins at a time, impressive when you consider the weight of a full glass.

Besides tents there were also carnival rides and games for children, as well as stands selling hot pretzels and roasted nuts; perfect for soaking up beer. Sticking out like a sore thumb was an enormous green mechanical robot dressed in an orange suit. It was probably eighty feet high, and kept gyrating its arms and head back and forth while uttering choppy, barbaric phrases in German. As an adult, I was frightened by the massive beast. I could not even imagine the fear it would have provoked if I were a young child. The Germans must have a higher tolerance for these sorts of things. After walking around the grounds for an hour I had to abandon Evan and return to the tent as I rapidly became sick after lunch. I never made it back to the festivities. I just rolled around in the tent with an upset stomach feeling fatigued and lethargic. I was in and out of sleep most of the night.

I tried to motivate myself to get back into
action the second day but was still feeling
shitty. I had no choice but to lay low at the
campgrounds until the flu passed. Meanwhile,
Evan went off to have fun with the girls in
town. I slept the day away in the tent, feeling mentally and physically like garbage. It
was disconcerting having to pay forty dollars
a day to lie on the ground while hundreds of
people were celebrating all around me. The
camp served as an interim party during the day
as campers came and went from the festivities
in Munich. It was not until late on the third
day that I was able to muster enough energy
to make it back into town. This was my last
chance to see Becky and Dee, so I dragged
myself along to enjoy at least one night of
partying before saying goodbye. After a liter
at the Spaten tent I started to catch a buzz
and come into my own. We transferred over to

the Augustiner tent early to secure a seat before it became too packed. The immense, sprawling hall was filled with hundreds of long wooden tables and benches large enough to sit about eight people per side. We commandeered a spot on the end of one of the tables and began swilling our brews with reckless abandon. The waitress in our section loved us. She was especially inclined towards Becky, kissing her all over the face and hugging her repeatedly.

While we skulled beers and made friends with the people around us, a polka band was wailing away on a raised platform in the middle of the hall, jamming on such classics as *Roll Out The Barrel* and *The Chicken Dance*. During the German songs we would sing at the top of our lungs pretending we knew the words, spewing gibberish the likes of Evan and Andy's gypsy tongue in Budapest. Every few songs the band would stop to lead a drinking chant.

"Ziggy Zaggy Ziggy Zaggy Oy! Oy! Oy! Ziggy Zaggy Ziggy Zaggy Oy! Oy! Oy! Ziggy Zaggy Ziggy Zaggy Oy! Oy! Oy!"

Everyone would hold up their steins in unison, and the crowd would "cheers" (prost) together. The combined energy of the thousands of revelers packed into the beer hall was tremendous. Looking out across a sea of madness and drunken joy, not a face in the whole joint was without a smile. Everyone in our immediate area was hugging, dancing, and passing out high fives like they were going out of style.

We met some hilarious people that night. A balding British guy sitting at the next table over became enamored with Dee's breasts the moment he saw them. Dee is a full-bodied girl. Saying that her boobs are enormous would not be doing them justice. I am not sure exactly what her bra size is… but I think its somewhere around double Q. They are her finest physical assets. She has no problem showing them off, readily allowing friends to squeeze them at will, blushing only faintly when they become the topic of conversation. In the case of this crazy bald dude, she was just fine with letting his buddy take pictures of his cue ball cranium next to her mammoth orbs. I think he even tried motor boating them. Of course we were all egging him on and laughing along. The only one who was not entertained was his wife.

Sitting next to us at the table were the coolest British family. The mum, Jen, was with her second husband Stewart, daughter Emily and stepson Neil, twenty-four and twenty-one years old respectively. Emily was a very attractive blond with a nice smile and sharp wit that I connected with immediately. Neil was a riot. He kept screaming, "This is the best night of my life," sarcastically at the top of his lungs. Jen and Stewart were incredibly youthful and jovial. I had never seen parents get down and bogey so hard with their kids.

When the shenanigans came to an end, and everyone began to clear out of the packed hall, Evan and Becky chose to head back to the campground. Our adopted British parents invited Dee and me to come back to their flat in town to share a bottle of wine. Stewart was a successful businessman and had a lovely second floor flat overlooking one of the main boulevards in town. Being the ever-hip couple, they handed us one of their bottles of white wine and urged their two kids to continue the party back at the campsite with us. I am sure they probably wanted some privacy so they could jump on the good foot and do the bad thing. They had been stealing kisses from one another the whole walk home. They were such a cute couple.

We hit the metro with our bottle of wine, chanting and singing, laughing and carrying on. The hordes of people fleeing back to their homes, hotel rooms, and campsites were all filed into the late night trains, causing a raucous scene. They were scores of middle-aged adults falling over drunk, munching on warm bags of mixed nuts.

It became clear why Becky and Evan had gone back together when I got to the tent. In the last couple of days they had become more than friends. Evan informed me bluntly that the tent was "unavailable" for a while. Now we would each have our own European romance stories to tell. In fact, when I left to go meet Heidi down in Italy, he stayed on board with Becky and Dee for another week as their relationship continued to blossom. They ended up dating from that point on for the next four years, living together upon return to Chicago, and then moving to Charleston, South Carolina for two years. Since the tent was occupied, there really wasn't anywhere to go for privacy. Emily and I just found a bench on which to sit away from the crowd that had gathered at the site. There were twenty or so campers who had returned from town and had not quite gotten their fill for the night. Most of them were Australians. You have never seen a collective people who know how to booze until you have partied with Aussies. They can go for days at a time with little else for sustenance. It is their finest collective trait as a people.

I could tell that Emily liked me, specifically when she leaned over and started kissing me. Although I was caught up in the moment and all the excitement of the evening, I knew that I was going to regret it if things went any further. It was probably for the better that the tent was not free that night, because

I would be leaving for Rome the next day to meet the true object of my affection. This was just a one-night liaison. The kiss was nice; Emily was a sweet girl. Under different circumstances I would have been all about her. Alas, my heart was in Milwaukee. We met back up with Neil and Dee and called a cab for them to get back to the flat. Everyone hugged and wished each other well. There was a tinge of sadness in Emily's eyes when we said our final goodbyes. The short, powerful interactions in life are often the most memorable.

PART IV - ROMANCE

"Sometimes it's better to travel than to arrive."

-Robert M. Pirsig, *Zen & the Art of Motorcycle Maintenance*

No more accurate a statement could have been spoken in trying to describe my feelings when I rode the train alone through the bucolic mysticism of the Swiss Alps. It was a totally surreal picture outside the window as we motored through the mighty mountain chains, winding back and forth amongst valleys of stunning green hills that climbed to meet the crested snow peaked caps in the sky. The afternoon sun lit the land on fire and the view was so bright and clear that it seemed to pop out at your eyeballs like a 3-D movie. Parallel to the track was a fresh, clean mountain stream rushing alongside, sending gentle white foam to the surface. Large weathered boulders presented surfaces smoothed by thousands of years of flowage. Occasionally we whizzed past small country hamlets, each consisting of a mere few Alpine homes. Behind the homes lay sprawling fields of pure emerald grass with dairy cows grazing happily. Intermittently dispersed pine trees painted shade on the ground below.

There are very few times in my life where I have seen something so naturally beautiful that it literally takes my breath away, but this was one of them. A few other times I can remember were the day I spent at Machu Picchu high in the Andes Mountains, standing on Sugar Loaf Mountain overlooking the beaches and jungle of Rio de Janeiro, and the view of the city and sea after climbing the Lion's Head in the middle of Cape Town, South Africa.

Matched with the excitement permeating my body at the prospect of being less than one day away from Heidi in Rome, I was almost quivering with delight. I could not believe the perfect alignment of the cosmos, how spectacular and supernatural the present moment was. The majesty of the landscape outside the window overpowered my eyes while the weight of infatuation for Heidi controlled my heart. I have never been that overtaken by joy and love at the same time. I was mad about the earth, mad about being in love, and overwhelmed by the power of my freedom. Riding the rails in Switzerland. Life was so beautiful I could hardly comprehend it.

In Rome

My head is spinnin' with words,
And I'm nothing but grinnin'
As today I travel down to Termini,
To see the pearly work, her methodical smirk,
It's been three weeks, but that's an eternity,
When I hold my chest and feel new burning,
Not sick, but quick, and sharp like a dagger,
For three months to wait,
And wonder if I could have her

Now the wondering is coming to a halt,
For a week, I finally get to speak,
With my lips, not the keys,
And she can believe I'm not pretending,
Its never ending, I'm bending all the rules,
About the way its supposed to go down,
I use this ink to expound & rebound,
What's already been laid down

No reason for doubt,
when your belief is devout,
Like a Christian, this my confession:

The greens I'm seeing in these mountains,
Are pale and gray when I think,
Of the ones in your eyes,
It's no surprise these words fly,
And I could write a book,
from just one look,
One stare, I don't care,
kick my teeth, pull my hair,
Just don't steal my reality,
I'll defy gravity, to get it back,
If you try and take it,
I can't wait to get to Rome,
So we can finally make it

Words flowed freely from my pen on the way down to Rome, anticipation growing exponentially by the minute. When I arrived, my first mission was to find a hostel close to Termini train station in the middle of the city. The next day I would be trekking to the airport from this station in order to meet Heidi at the terminal and bring her back to town. The place I picked from my travel book was perfect. It was close to the station and the people working and staying there were very welcoming. Much larger than previous hostels, these rooms held six bunk beds each and were full of people. At night they all gathered to drink wine and tell tales of all their travels around Europe and the rest of the world. It was the largest group of backpackers I had hung out with in one milieu, a hodgepodge of Brits, Aussies, Poles, Kiwis (New Zealanders), and Germans. They told wondrous stories about the places they had seen and people they had met. I began to feel like a member of an exclusive, privileged club.

Those who are passionate about travel have a lot in common. A certain mix of curiosity, open mindedness about people and ideas, and a zest for learning. I gained so much knowledge about other countries and lifestyles just by sitting down and asking questions. Unexpectedly, I learned much about my own country. The perspectives foreigners have of American people and culture are helpful because their unbiased viewpoints diminish our own inflated sense of importance. Being away from the incessant brainwashing that promulgates the idea that America is the greatest, "freest" land on earth sheds much light on how imperialistically we actually behave. Just because the American government tries to convince us we are the best does not necessarily make it true. To say that one country is better than another is merely a matter of opinion. Often times, it shows a lack of perspective and global understanding. Those very flag wavers who insist upon our superiority as a nation have often never left the country to explore what else exists.

Despite their economic means, most Americans have not traveled internationally. Less than 60% possess passports. Of those who do, many have only been on vacations to resort towns in Mexico, such as where our sizzlers were held. These tourist traps are almost nothing like the rest of the country. They drink cocktails and beers served by Mexicans who speak English. They learn almost nothing about the country itself or its people. Nor do they give access to the viewpoints that educated Mexican citizens may have of their misunderstanding neighbors to the north. Canada is widely ignored as a foreign country. We generally regard them as the quirky cousin up "der" who loves maple syrup, pronounces *about* as "a boot", and happily proclaims the ambiguous "ey" at the end of their sentences. We do not really cross the border to Canada to learn about a different culture, more so to see Niagara Falls, ski in British Columbia, or go fishing for Largemouth Bass and Northern Pike in Ontario.

Americans, especially fundamental conservatives, flaunt the red, white, and blue as a tool for the purpose of pushing ideas. Politicians use this strategy to mask their true intentions. Make no mistake; this is government propaganda at its finest. We hear from the President about the importance of protecting our national security. This is supposedly why we wage wars half way across the planet.

"Don't think rationally about the legitimacy of our foreign actions," the government tells us, just make sure you support us, because if you do not, that means you must hate freedom. If you hate freedom, then you must be a terrorist. Blind patriotism is the only way to prove you love your country.

The perfect example would be the "anti-terror" measures that were passed after 9/11 that essentially justified spying on anyone the government felt was "suspicious;" a danger to national security.

"We don't need to have justification for accessing personal data, wiretapping or using surveillance; we just have to tell the public it's necessary to ensure our safety as a nation."

Otherwise, these "freedom haters" might be able to plan another attack that would endanger our citizens. This is why the Department of Homeland Security spends billions of dollars of taxpayer money. You could not have walked through an airport in the States at this time without hearing announcements over the loud speaker that informs travelers of the current climate of fear; oops, I mean danger.

How am I supposed to react to an "orange alert?"

This is the most preposterous announcement of all time. How in God's name can the government assess the so-called level of danger in any given airport anywhere in this vast, expansive country at any given time with any kind of accuracy whatsoever?

And if we live in a land that feels the need to measure its security over loud speakers in airports, then is our country really that free? I don't hear these same warnings when I get on a train in Hungary. I can smoke a joint in a café in The Netherlands, but not at home. Isn't that freedom? In Canada, as well as every other "western" nations, I receive free health care if I am a citizen. Would not the astronomical costs of health-care be characterized as a societal shackle? I began to question the American definition of freedom, and what our basis is for claiming that our country is the best.

What do we take for granted when we are caught up and consumed by living our day to day lives, studying, working, seeking accomplishments and success? I would argue that one of the greatest necessities foregone is our need for introspection and reflection. When we step outside of our comfort zone, our routine, and all things that are usual and consistent, we transcend our environment and tap into a spirit of wonderment. Alternative thought patterns within us, that are often guarded or protected from our reality, come to the cerebrum. For example, sitting on a train watching the rolling green peaks of the Swiss Alps in late September, ideas and thoughts that I had never experienced would manifest themselves with utter clarity in my consciousness. Thoughts about how taking only two weeks vacation per calendar year, the norm in the States, is in actuality an egregious waste of your life. Europeans average between four and six weeks of holiday each year. Two weeks is barely enough time to catch up on the errands and chores that are neglected whilst you slave away at your 50 to 60 hour a week career, let alone plan a trip to detach your mind and refresh your spirit before returning to work. Why do we accept this standard?

Another example would be sitting at a café on the square of a major city like Prague, just watching people go about their daily lives, the urgency, or lack of urgency, with which they carry themselves. How their body language differs from that of Americans. The possibility of a casual pace of life rather than the "hurry up and do" philosophy. This ability to transcend my culture and my own mind was one of the most empowering facets of this trip. Evan and I were both enamored with the leisurely sense of peace the Europeans carried themselves with. We became aware of this sidewalk, café culture, embracing it fully. It allowed us to appreciate simple, meaningful conversation, or just to sit and think.

Some of my favorite memories are these moments pondering with our journals and a cup of coffee in front of us. The time spent exploring the processes of our thought, considering new paradigms, enumerating the feelings and opinions that came into our heads. Such fantastic visions manifest themselves when the foggy haze in our minds that guards our true passions wisps itself away compliantly. We can then decipher the coded thoughts within our minds. None of the familiar impediment thoughts are there to hold us back. This is the true essence of the freedom I felt throughout this journey. We experienced many of the wonders we had read about in textbooks in school, accordingly unearthing realities that we could never have fully understood from just reading a book. What only our minds could comprehend from those books, our spirits could drink in places like the cafes of Amsterdam or the majestic Coliseum in Rome.

The morning I was to meet Heidi at the airport, I found a quaint little hotel up the street from the hostel and paid for a room for one night. I figured our first evening back together would not be very romantic in a room with bunk beds filled with strangers. On the way to Leonardo da Vinci airport, my excitement was bubbling over like a pot of Ramen noodles. Upon arrival I located the terminal she specified and stood waiting impatiently like a kid at the mall in line to see Santa Claus. After about fifty people had deplaned I caught a glimpse of her blond hair hanging down from beneath her green military hat. She was looking all around trying to get her bearings and then stopped an airport employee to ask him a question, but made eye contact with me from over his shoulder. Her face lit up brighter than the Christmas tree at Rockefeller Plaza. She ran the remaining forty feet to me, bags bouncing on her shoulders, precious green eyes aglow, puffy cheeks rosy and alive. She leaped towards me with all her might, knocking me back in my tracks as I caught her. We embraced tightly. I remember how warm her face felt against mine as we held each other, laughing euphorically. Then she pulled back and gave me a giant, sloppy kiss on the lips. We looked at each smiling for about thirty seconds. Tears of joy were streaming down the side of her face.

From a tiny rural town in upstate Wisconsin, this was her first time ever traveling abroad. I hoped it was also the first time being this madly in love. I could feel the anxiety releasing from her body as we were walking back to the train. She released several deep breaths to clear the nervousness from her system. "I was freaking out on the plane," she exclaimed.

Not a person who sits still for very long, the economy class trans-Atlantic flight had been a formidable challenge. In the train car we sat next to one another, squeezing hands firmly and pushing our heads and bodies closer, not wanting a single channel of space to linger between us. She unleashed a spew of emotions that had been building up inside her whilst I was gone. I sat and listened, totally content to be soaking in all of her true unadulterated feelings. When we talked before the trip she said she didn't care where we went, so I took care of our itinerary. It was then I informed her that after taking in the sites for a day in Rome we would board a train to the opposite side of Italy at the port town of Bari. From there we would take an overnight ferry to a small, secluded Greek Island in the Mediterranean Sea called Corfu. "Yeaaaaaaaaaaaaaah."

I'm sure she would have been just as eager had I told her we were going to sit at the train station all week and hang out with the homeless people. She was ecstatic just to be there.

"We will spend four days in Corfu sitting on the beach, drinking wine and making love," I explained, "and then return to Rome the same way we came."

"Sounds terrific."

We lugged her over-packed bags to our small, single hotel room. Upon entering we dropped the bags to the floor and fell onto the bed in a lustful embrace. Passionate, ethereal kisses radiated energy back and forth between our lips as we re-explored one another's bodies. Every touch of skin, every trail of saliva sent the shock of a thousand nerve endings through my system. Breath was scarce, energy was high; time was meaning-less. Weeks of restrained emotion exploded from our mouths and bodies into the ether of the steamy room. Eventually we reached the climax of love, thereby exhausting ourselves on a hot, sweaty pair of sheets. Devoid of longing for anything other than holding each other tight, we drifted off to sleep with our wet skin sticking together, our whole beings filled with satisfaction. Waking up in the new darkness of early evening, I was in a world between dream and reality. Heidi's inno-cent young eyes fluttered awake and we gazed deeply into each other's souls. Our smiles returned to full expression.

"Hi," she whispered in the softest, most angelic voice imaginable. That night we went to eat some Indian food down" the street and returned to our nest to again become one and soak in the glory of true love. I never came down from the clouds that entire week together.

The next day I gave Heidi a walking tour of some of the finer points of the city, the Forum, Coliseum, Trevi Fountain, and the Spanish Steps. We dined in old-fashioned cafes, drank espresso, and ate Gelato (Italian ice cream). She was fascinated by the hordes of mopeds and scooters weaving dangerously through midday traffic. For me, the magnificence of Rome is that it's a modern city juxtaposed against the antiquity and splendor of ancient history. The grandeur of the two-thousand-year old Coliseum meshed with contemporary fashion, fancy boutiques and espresso shops is mind-boggling. There is nowhere else I have seen where the old and new worlds of man coexist so seamlessly. Most ancient civilization's relics are housed inside museums. In Rome, the buildings and structures that have endured over time are now the museums themselves. The Eternal City is aptly named. It's a hearty, indestructible monstrosity that scoffs at the challenges and pressure of time and natural decay.

The Roman people are a case study in themselves. Women who appeared to have just walked off the cover of a magazine were to be seen everywhere. Men with slick black hair, finely manicured goatees and sporty blazers drank espressos ubiquitously. The Italians have a natural, healthy skin tone, and their features shine. Rome is not especially known for its fashion industry. Milan, in the north, is considered the major hub for design and fashion in Europe. But the style and grace of the Romans is not to be overlooked.

The second night in Rome we checked back into the hostel so Heidi could meet some of the fantastic people I had met two nights prior. She was fascinated by the conversations and attitudes of all the other backpackers. We played cards, drank wine, and told stories for hours. I sat back and watched her mingle easily and naturally with these foreigners from all over the globe. Her enthusiasm was infectious and rekindled my own. Just feeling her presence inside the same room was satisfying enough.

Everyone at the hostel was friendly, but one guy from Australia, Julian, made the strongest impression. He was only eighteen years old, had just graduated from high school, and was on the road for six months before beginning "Uni," as they call college (short for university). He had a sarcastic, well-cultured personality many years beyond his age. Since he had no definite plans for his next move, we invited him to accompany us to Corfu. I was hesitant about the idea of having him tag along, but assumed he was an independent guy and would not be cumbersome. He was only planning on staying with us for the day of travel. No worries, mate.

I liked Julian, and enjoyed his charming accent, but he, like many Australians, had a certain propensity for exaggerated story telling. He tried to convince me that the very attractive Polish girl staying in our room had woken him up in the middle of the night to have sex. It was not very likely as there were eight people in the room that night. Heidi and I had to sleep in separate beds because the bunks were not sturdy enough to hold two people. It was frustrating considering how little time we would have together.

There we were, three lusty wanderers, departing from Rome with visions of tropical breezes and cerulean seas awaiting us on the isolated beaches of the glorious Greek Isles. I was happy to be getting away from big cities and their concomitant congestion. It would be great to lie in the sun, immersed in peace and quiet with my love by my side. A two-hour train ride east dropped us in the port town of Bari. We took a cab to the pier to meet the overnight ferry. The dusky sky turned to pink as the sun dipped carelessly over the Mediterranean Sea. A thunderstorm had just subsided, leaving a lugubrious, dark black layer of clouds hovering above the spectacular hues on the horizon.

Aboard the ship were mostly older men who worked for the ferry company. Gruff looking, gray bearded sailors sat around playing cards and drinking ouzo, a traditional licorice flavored Greek liquor, and smoking cigarettes. Walking around on the deck of the ship was an eerie experience. It was pitch black outside and a majestic wind had manifested after the storm. One careless slip on the wet deck and we would have been lost in the middle of the sea. We explored the ship thoroughly before settling down alongside the crusty sailors. We shared a bottle of cheap red wine while listening to the old men bantering back and forth in Greek and Italian. Heidi and I snuck into a dark, unoccupied barroom behind a maroon canvas curtain to fool around and be naughty. Afterwards we found a spot to lie down on the floor at the back of the passenger hall between two rows of chairs. It was bumpy, cold, and uncomfortable but we did our best to catch a few hours of rest.

Thankfully I had Heidi's warm body to snuggle up to. Any other night I would have been cold and lonely, cursing the wretched motion of the sea. I had never experienced seasickness before. These conditions were at least manageable, I would probably have fallen ill if they had been much worse. First thing in the morning, when the sun came up, we arrived at our destination on the west coast of Greece at the port of Igoumenitsa. There we quickly switched over to another ferry that took us to Corfu Town, the only port on the island of Corfu. The lower level of the craft was reserved for automobiles being transferred to the island, the second story for passengers. We sipped hot tea while observing the yawning, sleepy faces on board. Upon offloading, this time without the cumbersome blue backpack I left behind for storage in Rome, we met an olive skinned, extremely hairy bearded man named Walter.

At first I thought he might be a talking gorilla, due to the tufted brown clumps of hair on his forearms and bushy beard. But no, he turned out to be a person. He and his wife Claudia were waiting patiently at the dock outside of their white Volkswagen van for prospective guests to their hostel. As long as we did not mind stopping off for fresh bread and vegetables on the way, he assured us we would enjoy ourselves immensely. Julian was interested in staying at a busier spot called the Pink Panther that was highly acclaimed by some backpackers he had met, while Heidi and I took an immediate liking to the casual confidence and warmth of Walter and Claudia. They appeared a happy couple and were extremely patient with one another. Both had been married once before and were now working on a second chance. Despite being well into their fifties, they carried themselves with the youthful zest of lovers freshly smitten.

Walter's face was one constant genuine smile, while Claudia had a knowing, provocative grin. It stretched wider across her face as she turned around in the passenger seat to ask us questions about ourselves and our own affair. We became good buddies by the time we had zigzagged half way across the island. Up and down the minibus moved through narrow switch backing hills, picturesque aqua views of the Mediterranean peeked out around every corner. We found out that Claudia did all of the cooking for the hostel herself and that dinners were served family style at one big table where everyone ate together. It was a unique, homey feature that reassured us we would be well taken care of for the duration of our stay. Already sold on the quality of our host's character, I was blown away when they informed us that we would have a private room with a double bed overlooking the bay, a balcony jetting out over the beach below, homemade breakfast and dinner, and a private bathroom for only twenty Euros a piece. We had just paid twenty-five Euros each to sleep on bunk beds with zero amenities in the middle of the city. I could not have been more thrilled.

When we arrived at the hostel we fell in love with it instantly. The entrance led into a commons area that consisted of an open, sprawling dining room with an expansive patio outside and a cozy little bar against the inside wall. The spacious commons was filled with wooden tables and chairs that were later pushed together to form one large table for dinner. Fully exposed to the breezy Mediterranean air, the building sat perched at the top of a cliff overlooking the sea. Walking through the doorway opposite the entrance led us outside, down to the bedrooms and dorms. Beyond the buildings was a dirt path descending through the wild foliage toward the water. At the bottom lay a secluded beach that stretched about a quarter mile from end to end. At night the moon hovered above the bay, sending simmering white splashes of light across the calm surface. Our clean, white tiled bedroom with French doors opened up to a breathtaking view of the cove. A large double bed with a sturdy varnished wood frame sat in the middle of the room. Our own personal bathroom and shower were tucked in neatly beside.

We could hardly tear off our clothes and get into our swimsuits fast enough. The arduous, lengthy journey to get here left us sweaty and dirty. We ran down to the water to freshen up. I howled a victorious yell as I crashed into the sea. The afternoon sun was shining down majestically on my bare skin, the cool water refreshing and invigorating. For the next few hours we lounged on the beach, reading, sun tanning, and being happy. There were maybe thirty or forty other people, thus ample room to throw a Frisbee we had found up in the bar. A few stray dogs were milling around as we tossed the disc. One of the friendlier scraggly mutts started chasing it back and forth as we threw. I would fake a throw one way, then toss the other. He was having a gay old time playing along. All was well and good until Heidi jerked the disc away from him playfully and he lunged at her, nipping the middle of her left thigh. From afar, it did not look like much of a bite, but it was enough to warrant a vociferous scream. I ran over to her and scared the dog off, inspecting closer to see that he had taken a serious chunk of her flesh. It began to bleed at a decent clip so we rushed up to the house and informed Claudia, who dressed the wound and calmed down a frantic Heidi. By the end of the day a huge, nasty bruise had formed on the surface in between where the two rows of teeth had gnashed. It was the only touch of gray to our trip. She was a good sport and did not let it interfere with our living dream.

The real pain in the ass, or thigh, in this case, was when she returned home to get a rabies shot and was informed it would require three separate shots in one-week intervals. Wanting to see her doctor back home in Northern Wisconsin where she felt more comfortable, she had to drive three hours each way from Milwaukee and back for the treatments.

At nighttime, Walter and Claudia retired to bed fairly early. They left the guests with free reign over the property. Although the temperature during the daytime had risen to ninety degrees Fahrenheit, the evening air was crisp and cool. The open-air ambiance was paradise. I threw some Grateful Dead onto the stereo and we drank beers from the community refrigerator, amply stocked with local and import beers. The hostel operated purely on the honor system. We were trusted to tally how many beers or sodas we drank on our personal expense log. There were two very cool guys from Austin, Texas who we met at dinner and hung out with in the evening. They were playing guitar and drinking on the patio. We talked about music and sang campfire songs together in the lucid autumn moonlight.

Walter's first son from his previous marriage, Apollo, was about my age and living back at home until he figured out what he was going to do with his life. He was a very calm, sincere guy, handsomely built with long brown hair, a clean-shaven face, and lightly tanned skin. It was comical to watch him lingering around the hostel looking so lost and forlorn. From his explanations and grave speech it was clear that he was caught up in some kind of existential meltdown, having graduated from college in Italy and not knowing what move to make next. The way he inhaled his cigarettes deliberately and exhaled them dramatically made me giggle inside. Not to say that I could not relate to him, having just come to the end of seventeen long years of matriculation myself.

Suddenly I was being thrust into this frightening world known as adulthood, responsible for feeding, clothing, and supporting myself with some kind of "career." I only had a plan for the next couple of years. I would continue selling books in the summer while full-time recruiting personal teams of students during the school year. After having drastically improved my sales skills over four summers it was my goal to develop my management skills. Recruiting would be a great opportunity for this. Beyond that I was not too sure.

The idea of locking into a job for the next five or ten years did not appeal to me. It was hard to relate to friends that I graduated with from the business school at Marquette. The faculty and administration were always encouraging us to find jobs with companies that could help "jumpstart" our careers. That seemed like such a hollow and meaningless end to me. Not too many people I know are intrinsically passionate about serving corporations. It's an idea pushed upon us by our colleges and universities that often glorify these faceless giants. I watched people taking jobs that required them to dress formally and sit in front of a computer all day in an office cubicle. What I saw for myself in that environment was a stressed out, unsatisfied thirty-year-old looking back at the last decade of my life wondering where it had gone and why I had not taken the time to enjoy my youth. Born an idealist, I choose not to give up on pursing a lifestyle I could be passionate about. Hence began my exploration for a job I could perform with my heart as well as my head.

At one point in the evening Apollo stopped the conversation to make sure we were all taking the time to appreciate the beauty and serenity of the brilliant, full moon. I was on the same track of thinking he was, having been marveling at its luminescence over the bay that night. I liked that he was grateful for how special this place was. We tend to take things, places, and other persons in life for granted. Especially amongst my generation, which has been pumped full of self-esteem and feelings of self-importance. The "Me" generation is all about self-realization, which is great, but we sometimes fail to take notice of the value of the ephemeral world around us. Really, it matters not what you have, but what you have that you are actually aware of and appreciative for.

A couple days later we met up with Julian and rented mopeds to cruise around the island. Riding along the elevated coastline we spied another larger beach with iridescent green waters and the faint, distant blur of naked bodies. I was giddy with excitement about my first opportunity to see a nude beach. We parked our scooters and meandered down to the water, peeling off our clothes tentatively and tiptoeing towards the water sheepishly. By his creepy smirk, I could tell Julian was going to enjoy seeing my girlfriend naked. As is commonplace on nude beaches, most of the denizens were old folks with sagging breasts and tired scrotums. Heidi was for sure the most attractive female of the whole lot. Her taut, athletic body looked incredible in the bright sun. Her soft, pink nipples became alert as we entered the chilly, crystal sea. Floating up and down carelessly with our wet bodies pressed together, I took extra special care to savor the freedom of public nudity. I knew my own country's strict moral obligations would never allow for such liberated behavior. After a few minutes the taboo of being bare to the wind in public wore off and it just seemed natural. Why should we feel shame about showing our bodies to the masses when God made us so beautiful?

We applied sunscreen to areas of our bodies that had never seen direct sunlight before and soaked up the happy rays. When our stomachs started growling we got back on the scooters and cruised until we found a cute little roadside café. Here we gorged ourselves on crispy lamb meat and pita bread. It was also a family operated joint, the grandmother of the family sitting at the next table took great delight in watching us foreigners sampling the local cuisine. She kept handing us extra bread and smiling in our general direction. We shared a bottle of wine, a perfectly acceptable thing to do at lunchtime on an island. When it was time to go, we walked over to the cute little granny and I took an adorable picture of Heidi and Julian standing on either side of her kissing her on the cheeks. She had an ecstatic childlike grin on her face and kept saying, "Nice Americans," as if petting a cooing kitty cat. That might have been the only phrase she knew how to say in English, but we regarded the compliment highly. We left the café feeling satiated and loved. The Greeks lived up to their reputation of being gracious hosts.

At the end of the afternoon we followed the rolling hills down to a beach where the sun was setting magnificently over the water. Salubrious orange hues exploded across the sky as Helios bowed his head graciously. Heidi was walking around collecting seashells while Julian and I played in the sand. Her sudden burst of introspection led me to believe something was wrong. She admitted to having some heavy thoughts in her head but was reticent about sharing. Back at the hostel I encouraged her to open up. It was then she told me a very intense story about her last boyfriend. It was not a happy one. She shared candidly about their relationship, which began back in high school. They grew up in a remote rural area without much to do for recreation. Their group of friends starting getting into drugs, sometimes going on two or three-day benders when her parents were out of town. It was not just smoking pot either; they were fucking around with some pretty serious shit. None of her family or teachers suspected anything because her grades were always excellent and she was a star athlete on the softball and basketball teams.

Eventually she went off to college at Winona State on the West side of the Mississippi River in Minnesota. Her boyfriend Tyler was already studying Biochemistry so she joined him and they lived together happily, for a while. Apparently the drugs were more than just recreation for him, rather an escape from some serious depression and angst that were only escalated by the abuse. One night at a wedding reception for a friend he began to get aggressive with her. They left in his car and were driving home, mightily drunk and high on whatever else, when he totally lost control. He thought she had been flirting with someone at the party. After worsening to a full-blown tirade that involved crying incessantly and thrusting his fist through the windshield of the moving car, he reached over and hit her in the face. This was more than enough for Heidi, who got out of the car in the middle of nowhere. He drove off abandoning her on the side of the road.

She chose to move out of their place imme-diately following the incident. After finish-ing up the rest of the semester she returned back home. A few weeks later Tyler's mother called to tell her he had been found dead that morning. There was no clear answer as to whether it was a suicide or if he simply overdosed. Whatever the case, it was a great enough scare that she knew she had to quit using right away. Like me, she has an addictive personality, but could quit drugs and smoking cigarettes at the drop of a hat. We are talking about a very stubborn, prideful girl here. That's part of the reason why she was so successful selling books. When she decides to do something, she goes balls to the wall and does not look back.

The weight of her past had been playing heavily into her feelings about me. Not wanting to scare me away with her horror story, she was holding a lot inside that had been burdening her heart. This was an opportunity to lighten her load and come clean about the past that was holding her back from being completely present in the moment with me. I sat and listened to the whole ordeal without judgment, but was very much shocked, feeling sorry for all of her pain. I could not image how much stress that must have been causing. I was just relieved that she felt relieved after telling me. It was the first serious conversation we had had and her trust to be totally vulnerable to me was reassuring.

As a result of this trip I was even more so in love with Heidi than before. We always had fun together and it came very easily. Our freethinking, free acting personalities were a solid match. At the end of the four days in Greece, neither of us wanted to leave. However, we paid our tab at the hostel, bid our new friends goodbye and boarded another ferry back to the boot country. On this trip, the boat arrived at Brindisi, another port city just up the coast from Bari. It left us with a four-hour layover until the next train to Roma. Being a Sunday morning, there was not much to do but walk around at the park and watch boats at the harbor. Seated together on a bench facing the dock, Heidi cuddled up to my side, leaned over, moved aside the hemp necklace she had made me on the car ride back from California and kissed my warm, sweaty neck. Shivers went down my spine as I turned to stare into her mischievous green eyes. I met her moist lips with my own and thanked her for taking the leap of faith in meeting me in a faraway land. I let her know that our time together had been the best of my whole trip and that I could not wait to see her in a month back in Milwaukee.

Before boarding the train in Brindisi we met another impressive young backpacker from Canada named Chrissy. She was only eighteen, the same as Julian, whom we had left behind in Corfu. I found her to be very courageous, a young female out on her own. She had a good head on her shoulders and actually preferred traveling alone because it forced her to meet new people instead of staying in a comfort zone with friends. She also preferred to stay out of the cities to avoid the craziness. Her adventurousness and self-confidence were an inspiration.

The train car on the return trip was empty except for a few other people who got off at a stop about half way into the two-hour ride. Once the conductor passed through and checked our tickets, Heidi turned to me with a provocative smile. She was wearing a skirt and clearly had trouble on her mind, the good kind of trouble. She started kissing me softly. Before I knew she was reaching over to unzip my pants. Her smile was provocative and naughty as she pulled my little friend, who was up to the task, from between the zippers. She then crawled up on top of me, her knees facing the window and butt on my lap. I slid my hand up her smooth tan thighs and felt her warmth through the thin white cotton panties with marijuana leaves that I bought for her in Amsterdam. Sliding them aside just so, then sliding myself slowly and methodically inside her, we gasped together with pleasure. We continued laughing back and forth the whole time as she bounced up and down in my lap, hoping that no one would walk in and disrupt our surreptitious sexcapade. As the landscape flew by the window I lost myself in love. I was so incredibly turned on by the scene that I only lasted a few minutes before losing control and exploding onto the floor of the train. She sat back down next to me and we readjusted our clothes, sneaking wry glances back and forth, trying to act like nothing unusual had just happened. It was the perfect ending to an almost flawless week together.

Heidi's Reply

Things I am not used to,
Come out in you,
Thinking is like dreaming,
Its hard to believe I will go unawake

I am smiling, views whirling,
Worlds spinning about,
My mind is full of words to tell you,
But they won't come out

To share, do I dare?
Or will I scare you away,
Feeling perfect,
knowing you're worth it

PART V - THE END

The first thing on my mind after seeing Heidi off at Termini was to call home and tell my grandma what a wonderful time I was having. It cost about five dollars for a half-hour international phone card to the states. Grandma was at home and we had a terrific conversation. I filled her in on all of the G rated details of the trip. I could tell by her voice she was truly happy for me and to hear, most of all, that I was safe and happy. I was in a place of utter contentment, counting my blessings as I returned to the hostel to gather my things and check email to see where in the world was Evan Quackenbush?

He said he was also in Italy, in the Florence area, and would be heading to Interlaken, Switzerland in a few days. That gave me a couple of days to kill before meeting him. I decided that when I returned to Zurich, the only destination I could find a train for that day, I would stop in Luzerne and then continue south. The train was an overnight mandatory sleeper which cost me an extra 20 Euros, including a comfortable pull out bed with a breakfast of croissants, juice and water in the morning. One of my co-passengers was hounding me with questions about where she was going, presumably a town called Villach. She kept pointing to that word and the word Zurich, both written in her notebook. Her incessant, frantic imploring continued for nearly an hour. If she hounded me enough, perhaps, I might somehow start to understand her language. I shrugged my shoulders over and over again until she finally left me alone. The conductor on the train would not leave me alone either. I had mistakenly grabbed a seat in the first class car instead of the second-class ticket I had paid for. When he asked me to move, I found a seat in a different car, unbeknownst to me it was also first class. I wasn't trying to be cheeky, but he thought so, and took the opportunity to scold me for my mistake, twice.

At the stop in Zurich, my third this trip, I had a mere half an hour window to run into town and pick up another baggie of grass. I was still rolling cigarettes from a pouch of Drum tobacco I had bought in Amsterdam but was becoming tired of the taste. I do not always smoke cigarettes, but in Europe it's easy to pick up the habit. When waiting for trains, in lines, and relaxing at cafes, it helps pass the time. So many Europeans around me were smoking that I felt like, "If you can't beat 'em, join 'em."

I jogged through the pretty little city with my big backpack bouncing to and fro; fully sweating by the time I got to the shop. Unfortunately, they were already closed for the day. I had just enough time to hustle back to the station and catch the last train.

The station in Luzerne is located about a half mile outside of the city. I walked to a hostel, checked in, freshened up, and went to town. The main hub of activity here is concentrated around an ancient wooden foot-bridge that separates the commercial heart of the city. Constructed in the 14th century, the Chapel Bridge is the oldest covered bridge in Europe. Inside are paintings that portray events in the history of the town. Along the bank of the lake were the games and rides of a fall carnival, highlighted by a huge Ferris wheel next to the water. Adjacent was the massive Hantsmuseum, with its unique, drastic overhanging roof and glossy black windows. The roof is a thin, flat protrusion whose shiny bottom casts its reflection in a glassy pool of water below. From the reflection on, I could see the lake and the Alps in the background. This modern architecture stood out majestically in this well-preserved old city.

What captured my attention most was a carnival ride in the square by the bridge.

It was a circle of hanging chair harnesses attached by cable to an ornate round wheel above, spinning smoothly in a clockwise fashion. I would call it a swing-go-round, rather than a merry-go-round. All of the seats were filled with young children from about three to seven years old. When the ride began to spin they were thrown horizontally out into the air, round and round. I distinctly recall the pure presence of innocent jubilation on their faces. They were so excited, truly immersed in the wonder and spirit of life. Meanwhile grown ups around them went on about their lives unimaginatively and morosely. For the children it was pure ecstasy. I was moved by the simple beauty and joy of youth.

That afternoon, a light sprinkling of rain filled the sky. I bought some groceries from the local market and made dinner at the hostel, hoping to bump into some interesting people. Fortuitously, I was placed into a shared room with an extremely friendly guy from Australia. Nate was the easiest going Aussie I had met so far. We had a great time bouncing sarcastic wit back and forth at one another. We joked about how "tough and stressful it was to be backpacking through Europe," speaking caustically about how rough we had it.

I teased him saying that I didn't think he was really Australian because he was not hammered drunk all the time. Nate was one of the many Aussies I met who had lived and worked in London for six months to save enough money to travel for the remainder of the year. Since Aussies have passport reciprocity with the United Kingdom, they don't have to worry about obtaining work visas. It's much more culturally acceptable in other western countries to travel than it is in the States. It's viewed as a right of passage and an enlightened way to learn and grow, rather than an irresponsible unfocused aberration of youth. Many Antipodeans, specifically Aussies and Kiwis, will take a whole year off between high school and university to mature before focusing on a career. I personally laud this mentality as it gives a person the chance to explore opportunities unavailable to them at home. Besides what seventeen-year-old truly knows what they want to do with the rest of their life?

That night Nate and I went out for only a couple of beers, returning early to get a good night's rest. In the morning, feeling rejuvenated, I set out to explore the city. There was plenty to see. First, I found a cool lion statue carved into the face of a fifty-foot granite wall. The defeated beast lay on its side in a nook carved behind it with a long lance through its vitals. It was designed to pay homage to the hundreds of Swiss guards who were massacred in 1792 during the French

Revolution. Next, I stopped at a head shop that sold hemp beer; brewed from the plant that produces marijuana. I found a bench on the waterfront, now on the opposite side as the Ferris wheel, and sat to enjoy a lunch of French bread, tomatoes, Swiss cheese, and salami. This had become my staple for the last couple of days. It lasted without refrigeration for long periods of time. I had spent more money already than planned and needed to stop eating every meal at restaurants if I was going to hold up financially until the end of the trip.

After Switzerland I was planning on spending some time in Spain, specifically the port city of Barcelona, the capital of social progressiveness and Catalan culture. I figured this would be the grand finale since I speak Spanish, the weather is warm, and the cost of living is comparatively inexpensive. Everyone I had ever spoken to about Barcelona, from studying in England to traveling Europe, had told me what a happening, upbeat, invigorating scene it was. There would be tapas restaurants with an endless litany of dishes, young active people of all nationalities, and clubs that pump dance music all night long. Likewise, the climate in the Mediterranean environs would be perfect this time of year. Currently I was enjoying the crisp mountain breezes being sent down to me from the snow peaked Alps.

Sitting on that bench after lunch, with the sunlight bouncing off the water into my face, the towering Swiss Alps lingering in the distance, I felt strongly that this was the most beautiful place in the entire world. The sun was glistening on the lake's surface in a triangular ray as the calming mountain breeze sent faint ripples toward me from the Hantsmuseum. Walking by were mothers with strollers, toddlers, children, teens, adults, and the elderly. Middle-aged folks strolled past, while the elderly would saunter and glide with confidence and experience. To my left was a sidewalk draped above by a row of hearty trees casting their shade, dead leaves strewn about on the ground. Another walkway in the sun lay directly next to the water's edge. To my right sat a short pier with planters full of vines flowering lavender and red petals, hanging daintily over the blue mountain water. I fed some swans, ducks, gulls, sparrows and pigeons. This place was just teeming with birds, a virtual sanctuary. The quickest most efficient of them all were the ducks, who became the benefactors of most of my breadcrumbs due to the alacrity with which they pounced.

Once I felt I had adequately captured the essence of the moment in my journal, I walked to the outskirts of town where an expansive stone wall had been constructed hundreds of

years ago, maybe to ward off invading armies,
I imagined. There was a path along the top in
which one could walk down its entire length,
as well as sporadic lookout towers that I was
able to climb in order to get the panoramic
of town. From the heights of the turret, I
got an even better view of the surrounding landscape. At the highest peaks of the
mountains in the distance lay a soft white
blanket of snow. Gradually as the elevation
decreased, the tree line began, and green
sprawling hills painted with coniferous trees
stretched across the horizon. Compared to the
mountains, the lake was just a puddle and the
people below resembled a colony of ants. I
tried to imagine how peaceful and happy life
would be as a resident of the heavenly town of
Luzerne. Brightness and joy filled my being.
I wanted to sit at the top of that wall and
revel in its majesty forever.

Making my way back through town, I stopped
at a church in the middle of a quiet residential street. What drew me to enter was
the sound of an organ piping sonorously from
inside. The church, whose specific Christian
denomination I was unable to ascertain, was
painted pure white with varnished oak pews.
It appeared that I was the only human being
in the whole place, although there must have
been an organist hidden somewhere. Maybe it
was a really talented monkey pressing out the

angelic, mellifluous tones. The deep, heavy bass notes rattled against my core, numbing my body as the melodic high notes twittered my ears harmoniously. I sat with my eyes closed in one of the pews while up above on the lofted second floor someone unseen played me a private show. Although the scene was devoid of a charismatic preacher spewing passion for the Lord, or reciting dogmatic quotes from the bible, it was a more powerful spiritual experience than I have ever had in a church. I believe it was a mixture of soaking my eyes with majestic natural beauty that day, basting my senses in God's glorious creation, and the ethereal organ music. I took a few deep breaths, cleared my soul of any guilt or malcontent that was present in my system, and walking lightly out the door; unseen and unknown to man.

Much enjoyment indeed was Luzerne. The crowd at the hostel was quite lively my last evening as everyone stayed in to cook their own food and lounge around talking and drinking. There was a very cool memory book at the hostel in which backpackers could share inspiring quotes, travel recommendations, and thoughts they had amassed throughout their journeys. One quote I really took to heart was:

"The most exciting time to be alive is when everything you thought you knew is wrong."

For me that did not necessarily mean I was finding things I knew to be wrong, so much as finding so much more that was right. I felt as if my head was being crammed with new ideas and realities that were going to stay with me. It was an undeniably exciting time to be alive. That's what I felt, very alive. A whole new world in front of my eyes, a whole new vibrancy in my bones. I felt like I had found my kind of people, those who wanted to learn about themselves through the world.

What I generally found with people I met traveling was compassion. Not only amongst other travelers but also amongst the locals. People treat foreign visitors with compassion because they can see themselves in those visitors. I concluded that we really do want to help each other and be right towards one another; it's just that our egos get in the way. Deep inside, people want to live true to the Golden Rule and "Treat others how they wish to be treated." For some reason, we find this easier with strangers than our own neighbors. When we see someone out of his or her element, lost or struggling with our language, our inherent instinct is to help. When we see one of our own, we often neglect the fact that they need compassion too.

I am not saying that everyone is extremely friendly to Americans in Europe, or anywhere else in the world, specifically those who advertise their nationality blatantly and arrogantly. But more accurately, on a person-to-person basis, people were kind. I became aware of a certain sense of warmth I was not feeling back home. I think that being in such a hurry all the time and treating people as a means to an end, rather than individuals, is a tendency all too familiar. I love my country and its people, but sometimes I get treated better when I leave.

Interlaken is not exactly off the beaten path as far as backpackers are concerned. Located in the middle of Switzerland, amongst the highest reaching peaks of the Alps, it is widely known as the Mecca for extreme sports enthusiasts. Skydiving, white water rafting, paragliding, cliff diving, biking, hiking, and any other outdoor sports imaginable are readily available. With two large hostels on the same street only a few hundred yards away, it's the ideal place to gather and meet cool, adventurous travelers. The spot I chose, the Funny Farm, greatly resembled the hotel on the movie *The Shining,* sans creepy possessed child and horrible axe murderer. It's a 1970's Swiss lodge hotel with an open foyer and a carpeted staircase leading up to dorm rooms on the second floor. A large communal parlor room with a fireplace greeted me upon entering. There was a turntable set up in the parlor playing cozy mood music while some of the visitors who had gone skydiving that day were chatting energetically about their experience. I felt immediately at home, dropping my bags upstairs in the dorm room and hurrying down to meet everyone. A couple of jumpers had paid the extra fee to have a video made of their dive. The movies included the whole process from suiting up, take-off, flight, and then the leap of faith. They were all professionally filmed and edited with upbeat music. I sat quietly but excitedly feeding off everyone's energy, living vicariously through the videos.

There were more American travelers in Interlaken than I had met anywhere else, and they all had great stories and attitudes. The coolest American guy I met the entire trip, besides Andy, was a dude named Tom Grise, from Connecticut. He was the same age and had just received his degree in Engineering from the University of Colorado in Boulder. Tom is also an avid Grateful Dead fan and possibly the only person I have ever met who is more sarcastic than me. It was a pleasure. He stands well over six feet tall with light blond hair, red cheeks, and an eternal permagrin. We clicked immediately, spending the rest of the night cracking jokes and hanging out with a few girls he was traveling with. In the morning, he and these girls were going to take a hike up in the mountains and stay overnight at a barn hostel in Gimmelvald. They said they would return in two days.

After contemplating for awhile I came to a decision on whether to sky dive or do a cliff jump, which apparently was more frightening. I knew there would be other opportunities for skydiving, but leaping straight off the side of a steep cliff was less probable. Also, it was twenty dollars cheaper. Sold. The moment I committed to the jump, the adrenaline began pumping.

The guys that came along with me were hilarious. They stood 6'6' and 6'8', and were professional volleyball players from Canada. Standing next to them I look like a little kid. Very chill, good spirited guys, they kept quoting lines from the hockey movie *Slapstick*.

"Let's really try and win this one guys."

Considering we were on our way to risk death by jumping off a cliff, this was comfortingly comical. Two girls from the hostel also came along to watch. The American girl, named Kelly, was really groovy. She had straight dark brown hair, fair Irish skin with light freckles, and a constant happy smile. We had a good rapport, as she was quite sarcastic herself.

The minibus ride to the gorge was full of laughs and good vibes. Anticipation built gradually as we weaved through the mountains, the road becoming steeper and steeper. At one point on the drive we had a view of an exquisite emerald valley sprawled between two mountain peaks. The scale of the open fields tucked in that pass gave me perspective on how small we are in comparison with this enormous ball of fire and mud we call earth. The hour-long drive flew by and before I knew it, we were stopped and unloading our gear.

I wasn't really sure what I was getting myself into until we arrived at the site and found two massive cliffs about three hundred feet in height staring at each other proudly. Down below, a rushing Alpine stream of maybe thirty feet in width raced mightily between them. At the top of the gorge was a metal platform that had been built into the rock wall on our side of the divide. Across the top of the expanse hung a thick wire line that was to be the support hinge for our chord. Wearing a harness clasped to a stretchy rope, we were hooked up to the wire line, with the rope hanging slack below. After a two hundred foot free fall, the rope would catch on the wire and swing the jumper back and forth through the gorge. When their momentum had slowed enough, they would grab a rope stretched across at the base to pull themselves safely to the opposing shore. The guys running the show were New Zealanders with endearing personalities and encouragingly calm demeanors.

However, they were so extreme about the adventure that I questioned their sanity. They handed us a disclaimer to sign that was basically a big joke to get you laughing before you jump, saying that if you were to die attempting this jump, they would not be liable for your death. It was unlike any waiver I had ever signed before, using blatantly direct vocabulary. "If the rope should snap and you fall in the river, landing in a pile of broken bones that floats away down the river, *So and So Adventure Company* shall not be responsible for your free-willed decision." I got a giggle out of it but asked him seriously if that would hold up in court, he said, "No, if anybody died we would probably all go to jail, mate."

His cavalier attitude about the risk gave me confidence that he knew what he was doing. Kiwis carry themselves fearlessly and their accents are reassuring. That was enough for me.

This being said, it's one thing to have faith that you are not going to die on any given day, and another thing to throw yourself off a ledge from two and fifty feet from the ground. The platform was made of metal grating with small holes cut in the bottom. You could not only see directly down into the vast nothingness of the gorge, but also clearly hear the raging river below. The guide, Dave, instructed us that the best way to take it was in two casual steps, leaping off directly out in the sky, so as to avoid any catching of the rope or jerky landings. This was nothing like bungee jumping, where a stretchy rubber chord gradually slows you down to a certain point, pulling you back into the air. This was a straight two-hundred-foot fall with a rope that catches your body as it's falling, sending it into a pendulum swing. That means there is a steady jerk when the rope actually catches.

The Kiwis tell us the second time is definitely the most nerve wracking because you know what you are in for. Falling at 9.8m/s squared, with nothing but weightless air below you, your belly rips up into your throat. You fall for five or six endless, adrenaline-soaked seconds until you are abruptly yanked from above, thereby swinging to and fro over the rushing river. When it catches and you realize you will not be plunging to your death in the freezing stream, you scream the loudest, most blood curdling victory cry of your life. It echoes robustly through the valley, bounding back and forth ecstatically against both ear-drums. The pendulum swing is the exaltation portion of the event. Your adrenaline wave releases through your veins, shocking your system while perpetuating your buzz. It lasts for about five full swings, waxing and wan-ing a mere twenty feet above the river. Then the rope is tightened across the bottom so you can shimmy yourself over to the shore to another steel platform. The rope is unhooked, you get a pat on the back from a Kiwi, and then you climb down the stairs, free to walk away on your now very numb, bloodless feet.

I opted to let one of the Canadian guys go first, just to make sure it was legit, and then I made the leap. The adrenaline rush caused by the jump forced the memory of the roller coaster rides of my youth to take a back-seat. When we came down to the bottom safely, everyone was smiling and riding down the peak of their chemical overload on the riverbank. Each time someone would jump you got to relive it with them. Screams and laughter reverber-ated at the bottom. The good times continued back to the hostel where we celebrated our feat with beers. It was a low-key night at the Funny Farm. I kept fooling around with the fader on the turntable, acting like I was a badass DJ on the mixer. Everybody was having a chill time, talking about the day, talking about life, generally enjoying each other's company. Tom and his crew were up in the mountains so the party element was not there. We would take care of that when Evan got to town.

The next day I was to meet him at a small hostel he had found on the other side of town. So much had happened on my end of the trip since we had last seen each other. I knew he would have no shortage of tales to regale me with as well. I could not wait to find him and catch up. When I arrived at his place he was out to eat. I waited for almost two hours until he finally showed up. When he did, I walked straight up to him and kicked him in the nuts for making me wait so long, and then we shared a big man hug and started laughing. We picked up right were we left off.

Although we each had plenty to share, we were both in a state of shock from all the madness. Instead of catching up on all we had seen, we just sat in the shade next to a glassy stream in town and relaxed. The water was a plush green hue that radiated against the bright cream-colored alpine houses above. We smoked a joint and sat for a while, enjoying each others' company, sharing small anecdotes here and there, but mostly just being in the moment, aware of the subliminal experience we were both having. As much as I had taken pleasure in forging my own path for the last couple weeks, it was otherworldly sitting next to my buddy and companion, partner in crime, confidant. Being alone has its advantages, but there is no better way to travel than with your best friend.

Throughout this trip I noticed there is a great difference between tourists and travelers. Tourists are generally older, more economically secure, and prefer convenience to frugality. These are folks who travel in large groups, are interested in seeing only those sites that their travel brochures deem necessary, and prefer to stay on the beaten path. They are more inclined to book their trips through travel agents, buy expensive souvenirs, and take guided tours. Structure and planning are paramount to these types of vacationers. They develop daily itineraries and then check the boxes of lists of things they must see. Their luggage usually consists of fashionable suitcases with rollers, expensive leather handbags, camera cases worn around the neck, and yes, fanny packs. For my giggling British readers, a fanny pack is a belt worn around the waist used for carrying maps, money, and other small valuables. For my American readers, you may be laughing equally because of how silly these packs look. However, the Brits were laughing because fanny is a slang word for vagina.

Travelers are typically younger, more whimsical creatures. They tend to watch their budgets closely so that they can extend their trips as long as possible, ultimately avoiding the real world and career jobs. This category is where you find your backpackers, carrying weathered packs with sleeping mats and flag patches from their travels. The men usually wear beards and shower biweekly, the women have disheveled, oily hair pulled back in a ponytail. You will find them sleeping in hostels or campsites. They carry their cash in a money belt clandestinely tucked into their clothing, eat baguettes and cheese for lunch, and sleep in train stations. The name of the game is freedom and spontaneity. Often they will change their entire itineraries simply for the fact that they have met someone new with whom they wish to travel with. For singles this will often be a member of the opposite sex. The road can get lonely and many an interim relationship has sprung up in such circumstances.

Although both groups have similar intentions: having a great experience, witnessing the local culture, and seeing the fascinating historic sites, their mentalities and behavior are dissimilar. Tourists take vacations, either on their yearly holiday or during retirement. They focus on safety, eat in nice restaurants, and enjoy the finer aspects of the culture. Travelers take trips. Few of them have jobs to return to, many are traveling until the money runs out. Their outlook is broader than just seeing the sights and eating good food. For them it is more of a mentality of being on the road. The uncertainty and adventure are paramount, like a Jack Kerouac novel, the beauty lies in the free flow of events, the synchronicity. They are searching for more than just a nice holiday. They are young idealists. Call them dreamers. Call them foolish. They want to see what the world has to offer, to open their eyes to new experiences and to learn. Clearly we fell into the latter category.

Obviously these are all broad generalizations. Tourists come in all shapes, sizes, ages, nationalities, and mentalities, but we had a lot of fun analyzing the differences. On many occasion we saw groups of tourists fulfilling these stereotypes, standing out like sore thumbs, presenting themselves as targets for theft and ridicule. We did see our share of foolish backpackers as well. We saw people, often Americans, speaking loudly and obnoxiously on trains, voicing their opinions abrasively. Other times they would raise their voice and get agitated when someone did not understand them, rather than trying to speak more slowly and clearly. There were British lads on stag holidays absolutely pissed off their skulls, stumbling and mumbling through the streets. The sociological experiment of people watching included an endless number of independent variables due to the extreme mix of nationalities. Sometimes we would just observe those around us and try to guess where they were from based on their mannerism or language.

One characteristic we noticed of the large packs of tourists was how often they can be seen pulling out their cameras. They want to make sure they won't miss capturing everything they have seen on film or video. The irony is, more time is spent looking through a viewfinder and struggling to capture the perfect shot for posterity than is actually spent enjoying the beauty and wonder in itself. A perfect example would be inside of the Coliseum in Rome. Instead of scanning the enormity of the arena, transporting themselves back in time two thousand years to try and picture the magnificence of the spectacles that took place inside, (gladiators battling each other to the death, the Christians struggling to survive as lions and tigers ripped through their flesh to the roars of 50,000 bloodthirsty Romans) they are squinting in front of a Kodak.

Japanese tourists are especially guilty of this photographic indulgence. You can find them around every corner in Europe. I have to give them credit though for their spirit and passion for tourism. You will never see a group of Japanese tourists without gigantic smiles across their faces, giggling and taking pleasure in the act of vacationing.

It's impossible to stereotype an entire group of people, but tourists are more likily to behave rudely, expect everything to go their way, and demonstrate impatience and frustration when forced to wait in lines. Backpackers are more accustomed to the inconveniences budget tourism lends itself to. They are prepared to wait for things and are more appreciative of the people who serve them along the way. Travelers tend to move in smaller groups for efficiency while tourists spend a lot more time simply trying to reconvene in their groups.

Above and beyond all others, Germans are the best travelers in the world. Their efficiency, knack for planning, detail orientation, and genuine intelligence make them the most prepared race of people in the world. If you are ever unsure of what to do while you are traveling, simply locate a German. They will have an exact plan A, B, and C, of the cheapest, most interesting places to go, how to get there, and where to stay. It shouldn't be too difficult; they will probably be wearing black socks pulled half way up their legs with open toed sandals.

Australians are the most adventurous, energetic, and alcoholically inclined folks you will meet on the road. New Zealanders are also abundant, considerably so in relation to how few people are in their own country, four million. The rest of the backpackers we met were a hodgepodge of mostly Canadians, Brits, Spanish, Dutch, Scandinavians, Irish, and French. I tried not to hang with too many Americans but it became inevitable. I was pleasantly surprised to learn that the coolest Americans in the world are often the ones who have left home. These like-minded countrymen reassured me that there are plenty others like me.

That night there was a party at Balmers hostel, the largest and oldest in Switzerland. We got into some beer drinking to celebrate our reunion. Everyone in the place was feeling the vibe. Loud, drunken backpackers surrounded us on all sides. We slipped out of the party early to enjoy the peaceful vibes at the Funny Farm. Our dorm room was an endless cycle of people hanging out, smoking joints, telling stories, and laughing. I had sold Evan pretty quickly on doing the radical cliff jump the next day. I advised him to slow down on the beers so he would not be attempting a two hundred fifty foot jump with a hangover. Besides, the next night Tom and his crew would be back, and I knew he and Quackenbush would get along swimmingly. Tomfoolery was sure to ensue.

The next day I went along for the minivan ride in the big Volkswagen, soaking in the nervous excitement of Evan and his fellow jumpers. It was a bright, sunny day, rather than the ominous gloom two days prior. Spirits were high on the back road climb to the gorge. I sat back in the cut watching the others and chatting with Kelly, who had also come along for the ride. I was thrilled to share the experience with Quackenbush without having to stomach the emotions of jumping again.

By the time we got back to The Funny Farm that afternoon, Tom and his crew had returned and everyone was getting ready for the party that night. The hostel had hired a band to play down in the basement, a dark, dank room with unfinished concrete walls. The local Flemish band, called 4-Takt, was like a mix between Guns N' Roses and a polka band. They played upon a tiny fabricated stage in the corner of the hot, musty basement. The room only held about forty people, but it was packed full, with beads of sweat dripping down the faces of those dancing in the crowd. Evan and Tom got along at once as predicted. We dipped in and out of the party every so often to rest our ears and hang out up in the dorm room. I could tell from Kelly's demeanor that she liked me, which became more apparent after a few drinks. I was certainly attracted to her. She had a warm personality and cute laugh, but my heart was fully with Heidi, and I told her just that.

Later in the night I saw her hanging out with Clayton, a thickheaded Kiwi from the adventure company. I heard the next morning that she had gone home with him. It was clear the guides were taking advantage of all the female attention from the backpackers. They did such an excellent job leading tours and were somewhat like local celebrities. With adrenaline running high all over the place, it was no surprise that these guys did pretty well for themselves.

The band only played until midnight, so we retired back to the parlor room in the hostel to continue reminiscing with all the other travelers about all the incredible activities of the week. Tom was carrying a small travel guitar with him, which he busted out to start singing Grateful Dead songs. At one point we sat in the stairwell while Tom imitated Bob Weir from the Dead, singing his exaggerated whining, airy tone to perfection. We were in hysterics. His personality meshed so well with ours, it seemed like we had been friends for years. In fact, we stayed in touch for many years after.

Sadly, in the morning, we had to part ways with ole Tommy, as he was off to Cinque Terre, Italy. We had one last toke and promised to keep in touch. Most of the people we had been hanging with were taking off that day. We figured it would be nice to get out of town and go for a hike up in the mountains. There was a barn hostel up in Gimmelvald that Tom talked about. We would spend a night there and return to Interlaken the following day before setting off for Spain. I was looking forward to getting away and seeing a new perspective high in the Alps.

We arrived at the station well early before the next train. Abnormally, there was a computer inside this fancy train station. I decided to check my email, unaware of how fateful an occurrence this would be. When I opened my inbox I saw that my older sister Lauren had written to inform me that my grandmother had just had a stroke the night before and was not going to survive. All I could do was sit there speechless and breathless, shocked to my core and sick to my stomach. After a moment's pause I turned to Evan and said as calmly as I could, "My grandma had a stroke, I need to go home."

In that very instant I knew that my trip had just ended and that I had to find the first plane possible back to the states to be with my family. She had not yet passed, but Lauren made it sound as if the damage had been irrevocable and that she would soon be gone. Evan was very supportive in walking back to the hostel with me and helping get my things together before leaving.

Despite being rattled by the unexpected turn of events, the walk back with Evan was quite peaceful. Having just spoken to grandma three days prior, we had shared a special twenty minutes. She could feel my happiness, and I could feel how much she loved me, wishing for nothing more for my life than pure bliss. In later days I would reflect back to the time we had together. I could honestly say that I had no regrets about our relationship. Sure I had let her down a couple of times growing up, but I had been wise enough to realize how special of a person she was, that her presence in my life would only be temporary. I thought of how grateful I was to have been able to spend so much time not only growing up as a child, but also as an independent teenager. Few people I knew had the same kind of relationship with their grandparents. Likewise, I had prepared myself previously for how I would deal with this sort of loss emotionally when it happened.

Before the summers of selling books, one of the emotional preparations our manager Chris Fugman recommended to cope with the many challenges of the job was to visualize such hardships as car accidents, friends quitting early, even the loss of a loved one. By picturing these horrific occurrences of loss and pain ahead of time and deciding what course of action to follow, it was much easier to handle them practically amidst a whirlwind of emotion. Therefore I had a sense of calm and clarity. Everything was out of my hands except for getting home to be supportive for my family and saying goodbye to Grandma. Her blessed, loving soul was already on its way to heaven.

In many ways, that walk to the hostel was the culmination of this whole story. It began with Evan and I on an unassuming road trip in the Smokey Mountains over a year prior, and was coming to an end here on the sidewalks of Switzerland in the Alps. Speaking to Evan years later he said, "The only sad thing about reading this story is that I know I will never experience anything so great in my entire life."

There is truth to that statement for me as well. As with any high in this life, natural or chemical, it is only temporary. Eventually we must come down to reality. It applies in the same way as gravity. But for just once in this life, at least, I believe that we were able to transcend gravity. In the finite duration of the arbitrary definition of our "youth," we could achieve no greater climax. The alignment of many stars had to be positioned just right for this story to play out as it did. Looking back on this moment, I can truly appreciate how special it was. Even though I had just lost the most important person in my life besides my own parents, above and beyond I was feeling just right. I had a sense of peace that some higher power was taking care of things and there was no need to worry.

Using the phone at the hostel, I procured a bereavement fare leaving from Paris that evening on United, the same airlines as my original departure booking. In order to catch the flight, we had to rush down to the main station in town with my gear so I could catch the last train of the day. Evan wished me safe travels and offered peace of mind at a time when my heart was heavy. He sent me off with an understanding look of respect on his face, and an heir of compassion to combat my sadness. I told him to have an extra killer time for the rest of the trip since I was going to be unable to finish our journey together. This had not been the happy ending I had planned, yet the trip, from start to finish, had been pure, unadulterated joyousness. Instead of a wild rumpus in the cosmopolitan capital of Europe, it came to an abrupt end there in Interlaken, the backpacker's Xanadu.

On the train to Paris I sat reflectively, summarizing the events of the last six weeks, as well as a lifetime of unconditional love from my grandmother Betty. Through all the ruminations of my mind, I remained poised and purposeful. The greatest sense of clarity comes when we dwell not on the unexpected, uncontrollable occurrences in life, but rather accept them for what they are, and do what is in our own power to adapt. How could I feel sorry for myself at a time like this? Although the final leg in Spain and Paris would have been magical, I had already seen and done more in a short time than most people would be able to do in a lifetime. Instead of feeling sorry I focused on the positives and highlights of my time in the Western European arena. Soon it would all be a dream in memory form, fading evermore with each passing second. I tried to savor the last few moments of freedom as we sped northward across Switzerland and into Southern France. When the sun went down I became drowsy and slipped into sleep with my Discman in my ears, the Grateful Dead seasoning my ears one last time.

"What the fuck," I yelled internally.

I awoke abruptly to someone trying to rip my Discman off my lap and the buds right out from my ears. From the dim security light in the train I realized it was a group of three scraggly looking teens up to no good. I imagine they frequent these trains, preying on unsuspecting passengers bold enough to leave their valuables out in the eyes of scheming punks. I yelled at them and pushed away the one who had his hands on my shit. Most of the other passengers were nodded off, so the commotion woke a few people. The criminals snuck out of the car before I could grab anyone's attention that might help me in corralling the bastards and taking them to the authorities. As I sat back down I became incensed with rage. How in God's mighty name could these pieces of street trash dare come after my belongings when I was on my way home to bury my grandmother? Impractically I grew angry towards French people in general.

"The whole population are assholes," I thought.

Obviously my post nap judgment was cloudy. A few deep breaths brought my heart rate back to normal. Eventually I slipped back into my slumber. Not a half an hour later I awoke again to a jostling of my CD player.

"God Dammit! You have got to be kidding me."

The gall of these heartless pricks. They were at it again. I certainly should have learned my lesson and tucked my player away safely, but I never thought they would attempt to strike twice. Especially since I had made such a scene before. This time they got it clear from my ears and were off to the next car before I could do anything about it. I chased them through the set of double doors to the next car, but they were gone. When I returned to my seat, shaking violently, a big French guy sitting across the aisle asked in broken English what happened. I explained the situation and he said he would try and help me get it back.

At the next stop we got off the train and he spoke to the conductor about the theft. The three of us walked up the train in the direction the thieves had absconded. We finally found them and the conductor made them give it back. Of course they denied it at first, but I think the conductor read the fury on my face as a greater authority than the incredulous looks from the lying dickheads. My stare was so intense I was hoping it would begin to melt the flesh off their faces. I thanked the big Frenchman for assisting me, and continued talking with him until the end of the ride. I walked alongside him all the way off the train for protection in case they tried any shit. In all honesty I was hoping that my new friend would be so disgusted with their behavior that he would help me bash their heads in. I am not a person normally inclined to violence, but the few times I have had my belongings stolen I have become so enraged and vengeful I did not even recognize my own thoughts anymore. The same thing occurred years later when I was mugged in Rio de Janeiro, Brazil. I wanted these kids to feel the rage that was coursing my veins in the form of physical force. I know now that I am in a logical state of mind that it would not have done anything to alleviate my pain.

It took me a while to calm down again after the whole affair, a cocktail of sadness and anger mixing inside my body. At least I was physically unharmed and still had all my belongings. At midnight I boarded the red eye flight back to the States. The next thing I knew we were landing in Chicago and the sun was up.

By the time I arrived home in the sub-urbs my grandfather had made the decision to pull the plug on my grandma's life. She was in an irreparable state as a consequence of the stroke, and would never be able to speak or comprehend ever again. All the fantastic stories I brought back with me would have to wait until after she was in the ground and the final period had been put on her life. I remember kneeling in front of her casket, the last time I would ever see her. With my head down crying, I was devastated about the loss, but more so I was thankful for what she had been in my life. She had gotten to see me graduate from college, an achievement she was probably more excited about than I was. She had showered us grandkids with love and affection our whole lives. Her legacy would live on in our hearts forever. What regrets could I possibly have at that moment? Mostly I was just thankful that she had not had to suffer through an extended illness before she went. The stroke had come quickly and unexpectedly in her sleep. Rest in peace.

E P I L O G U E

Once everything was wrapped up with my grandmother's passing and burial in Chicago, I moved
up to Milwaukee to recruit my own team of
salespeople for the Southwestern Program. My
good friend Shaun Bartel, who had recruited
Heidi the year before, would be my roommate
and partner for the remainder of the school
year. The following summer we lead an organization of forty students into the great
state of Oklahoma. Heidi and I continued our
relationship and eventually moved in together
in an apartment with our friend Tony Kunkel,
also a bookseller, and his girlfriend. Later
we would deem the place "Heartbreak Hotel"
as neither relationship lasted the duration
of the one-year lease. After bumping heads
and arguing intensely throughout the autumn
months, Heidi and I decided that we would be
best to part ways. This was exceedingly awk-
ward due to the fact that we still had to see
each other at weekly team meetings throughout
the school year. Shaun and I were recruiting
again at the same campuses, my alma mater

Marquette University and Heidi's school, the University of Wisconsin-Milwaukee.

I saw Tom from Interlaken again on a trip to the East coast three years later. He invited me to stay a couple of nights at his apartment in the trendy East Village in New York City. He was a perfect host, leaving me his key while he was at work so I could come and go as I pleased. The price of rent is absurd in this part of the city. It was $1,200 for the tiny studio apartment. Finding a hotel for under $100 a night is like trying to find a whorehouse in Salt Lake City. I had to sleep across two sofa chairs and an ottoman, but it saved me a ton of cash. Everything was just like it was back in Europe three years prior. We bantered back and forth with sarcastic quips and played guitars for hours. I began playing a year before when Heidi and I broke up. The used guitar I learned on had been a gift from her, and had served as the perfect companion post breakup. It gave me a medium in which to channel my sadness and frustration about the failed relationship. That reliable old guitar loved me longer than any girl I have ever known.

As for Andy from Oklahoma, we have stayed in touch loosely. We hung out for a day when I was in San Francisco visiting Heidi and her boyfriend at the time. She and I were eventually able to reach a level of friendship and mutual respect after the initial challenge of our breakup. Now she is living happily up north in Central Wisconsin. She tells me she is blessed with a growing family and a life-style as a stay at home mother that is beyond what her prayers and dreams could have ever imagined. Becky and Evan's relationship came to an end, but she remains one of my best friends and now lives only two miles away from me in Denver, Colorado.

I believe that once you have been bitten by the proverbial travel bug you can never go back to a fully sedentary lifestyle. Once you fall in love with the adventure you will remain forever in its grasp. For those diehards who are affected by this metaphorical bug, life becomes more than a day-to-day routine, just periods of downtime in between the next excit-ing adventure or exotic destination. Of the two of us nomadic wanderers, I was certainly the one to catch the fever. Evan did move from the Chicago area down to Charleston, South Carolina, but did not continue traveling. He remained there and lived contently for many years in the old sleepy south, just miles from where the first shots of the Civil War were fired at Fort Sumter. For me, freedom, mobil-ity, and travel remain the driving passions in my life. Further endeavors have taken me across most of Central and South America, the

Caribbean, Southeast Asia, the Pacific, South Africa, and much of North America.

What I have found living back in the states for extended periods of time, is that my memory bank becomes surprisingly empty as time continues. Once I become established in a routine lifestyle, the only memories that stand out above and beyond are those that involve death, loss, and love. Everything else gets jumbled up into a single experience where the days melt languidly, one into the other. There are certain advantages to the sedentary lifestyle, such as sustaining relationships, participating in your own community, playing organized sports, owning pets, or just being able to jump in your car and drive somewhere. The missing variables are uncertainty and spontaneity, and those are what keep me on the road. Until I have found a career or a woman that I am passionate enough about to stay in one place, I will forever be in search of the next adventure. We are blessed with only one lifetime in which to see and do all the things we want for ourselves, to fulfill our dreams. I am extremely grateful that I have gotten to experience so much already. Hopefully I will be able to pass into the next world, wherever that may be, feeling that I have lived my life fully and extraordinarily, just how my grandmother would have wanted.